# Poetry Ireland REVIEW 115

*Eagarthóir/Editor*

VONA GROARKE

Poetry Ireland Ltd/Éigse Éireann Teo gratefully acknowledges the assistance of The Arts Council/An Chomhairle Ealaíon and The Arts Council of Northern Ireland.

Poetry Ireland invites individuals and commercial organisations to become Friends of Poetry Ireland. For more details please contact:

Poetry Ireland Friends Scheme, Poetry Ireland, 32 Kildare St, Dublin 2, Ireland

or telephone +353 1 6789815; e-mail management@poetryireland.ie

FRIENDS:
Joan and Joe McBreen, Desmond Windle, Neville Keery,
Noel and Anne Monahan, Ruth Webster, Maurice Earls,
Mary Shine Thompson, Seán Coyle, Henry and Deirdre Comerford

*Poetry Ireland Review* is published three times a year by Poetry Ireland Ltd. The Editor enjoys complete autonomy in the choice of material published. The contents of this publication should not be taken to reflect either the views or the policy of the publishers.

ISBN: 1-902121-54-6          ISSN: 0332-2998

PUBLICATIONS MANAGER: Paul Lenehan (typesetting, proofreading, pre-publication) with the assistance of Claire Brankin, Bryce O'Tierney and Orla Higgins

IRISH-LANGUAGE EDITOR: Liam Carson

DESIGN: Alastair Keady (**www.hexhibit.com**)

COVER CREDIT: 'Shutter Room' from *The Flooded Rooms* (2007), by Clare Langan

# Contents     Poetry Ireland Review 115

## Editorial

It is sixty years since the publication of *A Cold Spring*, Elizabeth Bishop's second collection, but nothing about its title poem seems to have grown creaky or stiff. It opens with probably the most famous line of all about this season, Fr. Hopkins declaring that, 'Nothing is so beautiful as spring'. It's a plain line, considering the poet, but he knew how to be direct when directness was required. Of course, he knew how to be something else also, and this first line is chased by another seven in the stanza that careen through aural hoops, spinning through assonance and image and phrasing with breath-taking derring-do. He was a poet to swerve between excess and the quiet minimalist of bald avowal: '… that blue is all in a rush / with richness', he wrote, sounding for all the world the way a Bishop line sounds, precise and yet supple; lucid and yet open to a sumptuous loveliness.

Elizabeth Bishop tags an article and an adjective onto Hopkins' title: not just 'Spring' any more, but 'A Cold Spring' now. The phrase kicks off the poem, and by the time we arrive at the final word (which, of course, was always going to be 'summer'), we have been through change. A change of climate, certainly, (from coldness to chill sunshine to warmth and colour), but also a change of tone. In the first stanza, the leaves are described in the kind of language one finds in a technical handbook: they '… waited / carefully indicating their characteristics', but that diction warms up once the poem gets through the windy gap to the second stanza, nudging from pure fact to something more speculative and image-based. I love her description of the sound of bullfrogs: 'slack strings plucked by heavy thumbs', and her way of likening the rise of fireflies to the bubbles in champagne. This is a poem that moves from plain fact to a register and vocabulary that teem with visual and aural energy. It shoulders its language, in other words, from winter into spring.

A fascinating notion, this one, of how to make language not just sound one way or another, but actually be it. In the case of this Bishop poem, this means language that doesn't just describe winter or spring, but that is wintry or spring-like. Witnessing the transformation is oddly transformative: I tend to feel a little warmer by the end of reading this poem. Perhaps it's the workings of a master-craftsman (why does 'mistress-craftswoman' sound so odd?), or perhaps it is something to do with spring, with how keen we are to be transformed, this weather. We are all anticipation, eyes forward, counting the extra minutes of daylight, leaping over the fences of months like Bishop's four deer. 'What is all this juice and all this joy?' writes Hopkins about spring. Here, then, with its Irish-language content chosen by Liam Carson, is the Spring Issue lit, as Bishop's fireflies, 'on the ascending flight'.

Winter is behind us, and we are on the up.

– Vona Groarke

Frances Corkey Thompson

CIPHERS

Behind the desk-top icons
that spring open full of yesterday's words
I have set, as background, an early Kodachrome.
We squint in the light. Skin is Donegal-salty,
smelling of the Atlantic.

I want to click a face into life, click
on the faces of my child brothers,
on the square young shoulders of myself,
on my pretty mother, her hair showing a first touch of grey,

but these icons are closed. Hieroglyphs,
they hoard old secrets, defy decoding.
No, come on, just look at how all of us
proclaim ourselves
so clearly.

Frances Corkey Thompson

TRAVELLER TALK

basically Machu Picchu ridiculous and then we did Lake Tanganyika
such a disappointment just so rude we virtually had to crawl literally
finally got on the M6 oh what part of Manchester my brother-in-
law's aunt had the same trouble after her hip best at the airport never
at the airport what rate did you get euros or dollars they don't care
do they

have you tried chewing star anise health and safety gone mad that's
what's wrong with the place now you must go to St Petersburg Panama
Canal actually met this really interesting couple no they don't bother
do they we have so much to learn from them he never tips on principle
absolutely filthy you wouldn't believe full of McDonalds these days no
never buy at the hotel always buy at the hotel how much do you think
no go on go on guess ...

... And why go north of Beijing? Don't go north of Beijing. Come south
with us. See the Terracotta Army, Three Gorges and all. Don't go
north. Basically nothing there. Nothing worth seeing north of Beijing.
Nothing at all.


        the noise of what is to come, the small silence of now

## V P Loggins

OF BATS

The umbrella stood upside down
like a bat, he could say, but not
like a bat exactly, more like
the thought of a bat, like the way

he imagines a bat to hang
from a rock ledge inside a cave
that he has never seen and will
never see, knowing as he does

that he will never visit such
a cave, being afraid as he is
both of the darkness there

and of the bats, well, being afraid,
he knows, even of his thought of bats,
what he calls imagination.

## Ciarán Parkes

ISLAND

A lake the size
of a small room

an island no bigger
than a single bed

when you set out in your boat
you've already arrived

to lie on your back
beneath a dazzling sun

so small you can blot it out
with one finger

# Thomas Pirkle

HOMAGE TO JEAN RHYS

The door opens and you are always there,
sitting beside an iron bed,
holding snow in your hands,
or the dark grit of somebody else's sorrow.
A soft rain has blown your hair back
against your face, and somewhere a clock is
beating time on a metal drum.
Still, the room is yours – the notes of all the scales
you've ever played are frozen in the walls
and your hardest, deepest nights are bolted to the floor.
A cup of pale yellow sunlight sits undisturbed
in the one window with its curtains drawn.

But have you forgotten the old woman
who comes in the morning to sweep out
the shadows, the moths and spiders left over
from the rain, the one who has never forgotten,
not once, to close the room against
all coldness and ruin?
Now the soft leaves of your hands are saying goodbye
to everyone, and as we turn toward the door – black,
we now see, with the huge infinite patience
of your self-regard – we remember the day
you stood at a corner of the woods in summer,
with the same sparrows perched like bullets
in the trees, and stepped out of your heart into a blazing field
of poppies, and wrote for all of us on the living air
the one story that would disappear
forever into the rest of your life.

Thomas McCarthy

YOUR BEAUTIFUL LIFE

Michael Longley, *The Stairwell* (Cape Poetry, 2014), £10.
Michael Smith, *Prayers for the Dead* (Shearsman Books, 2014), £8.95.
Pearse Hutchinson, *Listening to Bach* (The Gallery Press, 2014), €11.95.

Bells toll for passing greatness in the neighbourhood of these three
books. Michael Longley's exquisite volume is dominated by memories of
his recently deceased twin brother, Peter, while Michael Smith and
Pearse Hutchinson, those deeply embedded angels of a serious and
literary Dublin, have both gone to their eternal reward. They have left us
these last collections as final kisses upon our worried foreheads. I don't
know if Michael Smith was much for kissing, but certainly Pearse loved
his kisses, especially from the mouth of any handsome boyfriend. The
evidence of kisses is everywhere in his work. There is a very strong sense
from these books that very important friends have left the house late at
night, never to return after their final comradely embrace: though, one
must hasten to add, Michael Longley is still very much in the wide
vestibule of living poetry; very much alive and not at all a shade. But there
is such a strong, uncanny sense of wanting to follow the dead that his
collection works as a grand farewell not to the dead but to us, the living.
This sense, this effect, is deceptive, for Longley is still the great living
note-taker of bird life and bog life, regretting only:

> Why did I never keep a notebook
> That filled up with reed buntings
> And blackcaps and chiffchaffs, their
> Songs a subsong between the lines?
> — 'NOTEBOOK'

To which our only reply is: you did; you kept a brilliant notebook, in
collection after collection, of all the phenomena around you, from the
rare helleborines of Passchendaele to the plovers' eggs near
Carrigskeewaun. No Irish poet has been more faithful to his first deep
materials, no poet has been more consistent as an artist. Out of the twin
palettes of Co Mayo and the Great War, Longley has made exquisite
pictures for a Protestant gallery of imagination, of a sensibility more
complex than the average Irish imagination, yet manufactured from the
common dyes, colours and yearnings that are exclusive to Ireland. His
work is a confounding achievement of self-restraint and calculated

isolation from forces that don't belong to him; national forces that have
made other poets giddy and useless as artists. His work is precise and
intense, verbally and visually, in the manner of painters like Edward
McGuire or Avigdor Arikha. Like the wounded Arikha, he has been
painting himself all his life, except the pictures have been bog flowers and
scraps of ancient Greek. His first butterflies of language were caught in
the company of WB Stanford and this he has never forgotten. Stanford's
ghost haunts his method as a poet and seeps through his poetry like a
preliminary wash in a watercolour. To read his work is to touch a
deliberately made beauty:

> When I die I shall give them all their names.
> There will be many robin generations
> Coming into the house, and wrens and blackbirds
> And long-tailed tits will learn from the robins
> About the cheese-dish and saucer of water.
> I'll leave the window open for my soul-birds.
>
> — 'DEATHBED'

The second part of *The Stairwell* has been well flagged. By the time we
come to poems like 'The Stray' or 'The Birthday' with their painful and
intense grief we have been well armed. These lyrics are heart-rending
and technically perfect; their perfection works as an antidote to
sentimentality or easiness of feeling. They are not comfortable poems,
however comforting they may have been to write. The tone is still held,
reticent as rural Down, while Peter Longley is made to live again
through boyhood memory and the memory of war. The feeling in the
entire book is simply as perfect as this (from 'The Birthday'):

>               ... Oh,
> The infinite gradations of sunset here.
> Thank you for visiting Carrigskeewaun.
> Don't twist your ankle in a rabbit hole.
> I'll carry the torch across the duach.

A brother was never so beautifully remembered.

    The late Michael Smith was a force to be reckoned with in Irish
modernism, one of the last stone-cutters in a literary world of poured
concrete. Long after the others, Brian Coffey, Thomas MacGreevy, even
Samuel Beckett, had left the field, Smith continued building that
beautiful straight and narrow wall where 'Memory had wrought / its
awful magic with time.' Many of the poems in *Prayers for the Dead* are
linked and cross-linked with other poets, voices and languages through
dedications, memories and translations. This was Smith's modern life:

literature as a dialogue with others, literature as both translation of itself and version of otherness. His oneness with Beckett is in 'Library & Cemetery' ...

> The cemetery bell tolled departure time.
> The high gates clanked shut. The library awaited

... while that collegiate sense of poets enriching poets is beautifully captured in his poem – 'Tu Fu in Templeogue' – about a gift of apples from Austin Clarke's garden:

> 'This house cannot be handed down,' he had written.
> 'But my poems can,' he said quietly, 'even to the few.'

Smith caught the windfalls off the tree of modernism, leaving the orchard with his richly deserved fruit; fruit that would ripen through publishing early Paul Durcan, early Gerard Smyth, early Brian Lynch and late Patrick Galvin. Yet Smith as poet believed in the song as well as the thought, the poem as the soul singing: in 'We Are Alive,' 'The River' or 'Poet as Outsider' he celebrates various forms of integrity within migration, of survival through some inherent quality of the poetic life. Invoking Wilde and Joyce as keepers of a Manganesque flame, he writes, in 'Poet as Outsider': 'Their musicality was their defence / against the intolerable pain of unbelonging.' The act of writing, for Smith, was intensely private, yet no less heroic for its privacy or obscurity.

His life was spent in the company of greats; his poems have always set up their stall in avenues of greatness – thus, we find him in the dying room with Machado at Collioure, in the earth with Hernández, or fleeing with Neruda back into a dictionary when childhood deprivation becomes unsayable, knowing always that 'A play with words is a play with worlds' ('A Single Word'). Smith's career was such a blessed, crowded and busy life in literature, with whole worlds to be translated and unjustly obscure poets to be published, that one forgets the radical impulse at the heart of his writing; a real poetic gift, a lyrical impulse as lovely as Hartnett and a determination as steely as Beckett. His homage and recognition of untranslated others, the cleanliness of his lines, as well as a deeply felt solidarity with the poor, will ensure a permanent place for the work of this fine Dublin poet:

> That city has gone with its peopled poor
> who dwell elsewhere, scattered to outlying ghettos
> where needle and pill have replaced the old rituals
> of games and gods and saints ...
> — 'THE PEOPLE'S CITY'

The astonishing Edward McGuire owl that graces the cover of Pearse Hutchinson's last book is a brilliant and uncanny design choice. Hutchinson was something like that owl, or something like a creature invested with McGuire's luscious plumage. Forceful, domineering, opinionated, learned, Pearse Hutchinson was the bilingual guru of an educated Selskar Terrace and environs. His view of life was studied and exotic, his critical faculty was sharp and knowledgeable. People responded not only to his sense of style, but to his deep knowledge. He was a wonder, really, and seminal works from *Watching the Morning Grow* to *Le Cead na Gréine* burst forth from this fertile and prodigious mind. His being gay was only part of the loveliness of the work: "'Mrs. Hutchinson, one kiss from Pearse's mouth means more to me than all the women in the world'", the lover Maurice tells his Mass-going mother ('What a Young Man Said to My Mother'). The mother's path and Maurice's path were never to cross again, but a tryst with this spirit of poetry had occurred, a mythical Maurice such as one finds in EM Forster's fiction or Roger Casement's diaries: it is the memory that remains real and becomes poetry. Yet lovers have flaws, as Deesh the Indian medical student would demonstrate dramatically, crunching a glass eye between snow-white teeth ('Merrion Square, 1948'). In his memory of Bert Achong ('All Four Letters of It'), Hutchinson would get to the deep core of it all:

> I wrote your name
> on a high hill
>
> remembering long
> delight new-lost
>
> I wrote your name in snow.

An image of the handwritten 'Near the Grand Canal' (for Patrick Galvin) has been placed as an epilogue to this book. It is a revealing image, the blocked handwriting like a handwritten review from Douglas Sealy, full of art and discipline – one can see the boy in the writing, the poet with a parenting among printers and others conscious of graphic style. Placing it there for the reader is a stroke of genius, like the owl on the cover, but it does remind us that Pearse Hutchinson would have demanded that kind of finish, or flourish, of design. His was a demanding talent that called each reader to attention. One doesn't approach a Hutchinson poem badly dressed, better to be prepared and attuned. Dense and formal poems like 'The Abbot of Piro' and 'Sleepwalking 2' are interspersed with spare etchings like 'Milarepa' and 'Listening to Bach', but this poet's masterful command of the material is the single most powerful message sent forth by his last book. The way he circles around the theme of 'Near the Grand Canal', pencilling around material as the meaning of Patrick Galvin's life presses in upon him, thinking of James Connolly and all the lost causes, and then, this – a perfect evocation of the beauties of socialism: 'And then again I thought of the great beauty of Lily Connolly, his wife, when, not long before they killed him – and *he* was trying to console *her* – she cried out to him: "But your beautiful life, James, your beautiful life!"'

Billy Ramsell

THE CONTINGENT

Alyson Hallett, *Suddenly Everything* (Poetry Salzburg, 2013), £9.50.
Sheenagh Pugh, *Short Days, Long Shadows* (Seren Books, 2014), £9.99.
John Burnside, *All One Breath* (Cape Poetry, 2014), £10.

Alyson Hallett is a poet firmly committed to siding with things. *Suddenly Everything*, her second full collection, is marked by an almost Heideggerian determination to acknowledge the unbridgeable gap between human beings and the life-world we inhabit. In poem after poem she sets out to engage with the world's non-human and even non-animate components, while respecting or emphasising their difference from, and indifference to, the human consciousness that perceives them.

'Transparencies' and 'Rocks', for instance, turn the poetic equivalent of a time-lapse camera on the agonisingly slow transformation of a cliff-face into glass, on the northward drift of equatorial rocks to form the foundation of Devon's Hartland Quay. And this is a volume committed to perceiving in deep or ecological time, to remind us of how stones marvel 'at the briefness / of people, clouds, trees' ('Only Stones'). (These and several other pieces gathered here seem like most welcome shavings from 'The Migration Habits of Stones', a vast and open-ended public art project that Hallett has been curating for well over a decade).

But this obsession with 'thinginess' extends beyond geology. The memorably mantra-like 'O Rain' recalls Francis Ponge, that great bard of the *Ding-an-sich*, while 'Love Poem for a Shoe', despite its punning cuteness ('your tongue is sweeter / than Shakespeare's when my foot / is in your mouth'), bears an indelible trace of Heidegger's great passage on Van Gogh. 'Ram', a pair of aggressively sculpted haiku-like presences, reaches into the animal kingdom with its loving depiction of how its titular beast's 'bollocks [are] swaying in sunlight'. Such poems combine the alien and anthropomorphic to curate what Hallett refers to as the 'conversation / between feet and road, / / skin and sun, eye and stone and tree'.

There are occasions, however, when the dialogue falters. In 'Clarks Shoe Factory, Street' a pebble-like core of observation is encrusted, despite the poem's protestations to the contrary, in a mulch of generically nostalgic childhood recollection. The editorialising or explicit philosophising of 'Dark Matter', 'The History Makers' and 'Lines' sits uneasily beside deft sketches of the natural world. 'Cannot Unsun', meanwhile, is marred by the poet's rather self-conscious insertion of herself into the poem's conclusion as a 'restless traveller' walking 'towards the Idle Rocks Hotel / to meet a stranger in the sun-lounge for tea'. The collection is marked by a sense of spirituality that seems simultaneously both ancient and contemporary, epitomised perhaps by 'Transport', with its winning depiction of how the poet and a group of female friends gather on Exmoor to mark a modern-day chalk horse on a hill. But in poems like 'Earth Baby' and 'Future Geographies', Hallett arguably overplays the New Age card, leading to no doubt sincerely meant but undeniably trite declarations such as: 'The answers are already / inside us / and all we need do is listen' ('What We Do When We Stop Talking').

On the whole, however, *Suddenly Everything* is recommended for its relish in the physical, for the eerie richness with which poems like 'Came Creeping' and 'Liberty Bone' generate and enact a conversation with the fundamental otherness of the non-human world.

Sheenagh Pugh's twelfth collection is very much a book of edges and extremes, of limits and the liminal. Its opening poem, 'Extremophile', reads as the volume's manifesto with its depiction of bacteria, lichen and tubeworms that survive in various horrifically marginal zones. Its human companion piece is the memorable 'Pomor', which celebrates the arctic-dwelling community who survived 'at the world's roof' and traded across the White Sea and its environs, what Pugh refers to as 'the world's most permeable frontier'. ('Extremophile' would have made a better title for the book than the rather twee parallelism of *Short Days, Long Shadows*).

The collection centres on what 'The Sound of a Diamond Planet' refers to as, 'things not quite there', with pending or remembered arrivals and departures, with the state of suspension that arises from not being properly in one place or another. Such concerns are artfully reflected in the volume's structure, with early poems 'Come and Go' and 'Staying' finding their echoes in 'How to Leave' and 'Return' at its conclusion.

'Days of November 2009' hovers beautifully in the space between seasons, in the time 'before dark, / before winter' with its 'Angled light, always // on the edge of leaving.' 'A Good Sunrise' occupies a similar hesitant space, emphasising the incremental drift of night into morning, one marked by unspectacular, 'slow-growing light'. 'Different Corridors', meanwhile, powerfully enacts the transition between sleep and wakefulness, the efforts to snap or catch at the facts and faces of a rapidly unravelling dream.

The space between life and death, too, is explored. 'Terra Nova' recalls the poet's father's final birthday, describing how he watched ships sail out beyond Cardiff Bay. The parallel between the vessels 'leaving safe harbour / to seek the world's end' and the father's own imminent departure is simply but affectingly drawn.

Yet there are moments throughout this collection when one is left asking for more, somehow. A poem like 'What He Saw, Vesterålen', for instance, seems to taper off or exhaust its cognitive pressure when Pugh might have profitably followed its thread of mediation into darker, more torpid zones. Others like 'Big Sky' or 'Fogbound' seem to end prematurely, on a pat if undeniably well-worked image when their material could have been worked harder and further. But the deft violence of 'Gannet', the chilling 'Naglfar', the precision of 'Catching Up', these all remind us that Pugh is a poet to be reckoned with, especially when she doesn't recognise her own limits.

*All One Breath*, the latest collection from the prolific and much-garlanded John Burnside, opens with the Ashbery-recollecting 'Self-Portrait as Funhouse Mirror', a striking ten-poem suite that riffs on various more-or-less autobiographical instances of mirroring or reflection. (As a bonus, the theme is artfully embodied in the sequence's structure, the first poem mirroring the tenth, the second the ninth and so on). It's an ambitious meditation, one in which Burnside sets out to revivify the by-now surely clichéd trope of the double in Scottish literature, as he takes on the vexed questions of perception and identity, and the contingent, slippery nature of what we presume to call the self.

'That wasn't me', Burnside writes, referring to his own grotesque reflection, reflected *ad infinitum* during a childhood visit to a funhouse. Notions of imposture and usurpation loom large. In 'Self Portrait', for instance, the poet portrays his present-day, middle-aged self as a 'patient / look-alike' who's stolen the life of the hopeful adolescent he once was. Its companion piece, 'Self Portrait as Picture Window', positively longs for such replacement, the poet wishing that 'it isn't me at all / who stands here' but a better, nobler version of himself, a man 'so like [himself] that nobody / would spot the difference'.

'A Rival' treats the concept with a lighter touch, depicting how the poet falls in love with his wife's ever-so-slightly distended double when he watches her through a window: 'I catch a passing glimpse of someone new, / someone I might have loved had we ever met'. And in 'Return of the Prodigal Son', the dutiful, stay-at-home 'other son' seems menaced by the repentant spendthrift's sudden reappearance. But the most engaging and terrifying *doppelgänger* is to be found in 'A Couple', a riddling mini-funhouse of a poem that thrills and disorientates in equal measure.

Burnside is a poet with a bleak and unrelenting focus on his own iniquitous nature. In the opening poem he refers to himself as '[B]aby-faced / pariah; little / criminal', and there's rather too much of this full-throttle self-accusation throughout the collection, prompting the reader to ask how bad a person can Burnside actually be? But his *J'accuse* extends to the human race in general, to the 'public cheats and smug self-regulation, / [the] liars in boardrooms' that run our fallen world ('Spiegelkabinett, Berlin, 2012'). 'Nocturne: Christmas, 2012', a heartfelt elegy for Dennis O'Driscoll, picks up with greatest clarity the environmentalist note that echoes through the volume's final section, with its depiction of 'otters and sunbirds straggling towards extinction'.

It's hardly surprising, then, that a notable feature of Burnside's writing – here as elsewhere – is that the unravelling of selfhood is to be longed for more than feared. Poems like 'Devotio Moderna', 'Earth' and the powerful concluding 'Choir' celebrate the dissolution of body and mind, relishing how we meld with and melt into the earth, how the living and the dead are *all one breath*. Despite the off-notes of grumpiness and self-aggrandisement, then, All One Breath is to be welcomed as a jagged and weathered milestone on a singular poetic journey, one distinguished by writing of philosophical seriousness, rigorous self-examination and a densely sensual devotion to the natural world.

## Martin Monahan

THE KULESHOV EFFECT

1.
The lone object is neutral; yet in relationship
with another image, meaningful. Bleeded, transposed
or intensified. The syntax is not linear, as in prose,
but multi-directional; the semantics unfixed.


    1.1.
    A grey sky / three men sit in a cab
    a grey sky / cityscape of Petrograd
    a grey sky / waving women looking happier
    a grey sky / a climbing brick-carrier


2.
We project our feelings onto contiguous
shots. Our eye-lust for the pretty sitting girl
sees expressionate lust in the watching actor. The radial
content unfurls without a definite circumference.


    2.1.
    A green bench / inset a photocopied document
    a green bench / Nevsky Prospect apartment
    a green bench / a criminal in a choking fit
    a green bench / an eyewitness composite


3.
The consequence of this effect in actuality
is so little needs to be an overt explication;
viewers will just expand upon correlation –
their minds jewelling a thousand unique causalities.

3.1.
A red apple / caterpillar chrysalis
a red apple / the sun in half-eclipse
a red apple / then a butterfly pressed to a page
a red apple / Pulkovo airport baggage signage


4.
Despite auteur intention, montage might just remain
no more than bricolage: we make of it what we will!
And though most associations are predictable,
at times they'll flower quite brilliant and strange.


4.1.
A white petal / potholed asphalt
a white petal / pavements lined with salt
a white petal / rain puddled gasoline
a white petal / cut to a cinema screen

Monica Corish

WING MIRROR, BUTTERFLY
  – for Nancy McNamara

In the first silence of this frantic day
I hear the rattle in your lungs, grown louder,
stronger. I know you could die like this,

drowning. I know I can manage
your distress with morphine.
But Dad? My aunt? My brother,

on the road from Dublin? My sisters,
flying in from London?
I don't want them to hear you die like this.

I ring the Hospice, beg the night nurse:
*I have ampoules of Buscopan in the house*
*to dry her up, but no needles or syringes.*

*Can you give me needles and syringes?*
I clip a wing mirror driving through the village.
She talks me through doses, frequency,

how to insert a sub-cutaneous butterfly.
I drive home, pierce your skin with the tiny needle,
inject the Buscopan. Wait an hour.

Your breath becomes, briefly, a little less wet,
less loud; a little less
like drowning.

Eoghan Walls

AN X-RAY VISION ON THE TRAIN TO GLASGOW

I wanted to see the tattooed rose
trickling under your underclothes,
how wild you let your vulva grow,
if your lips were salmon or indigo,
but I glanced on my own soft dough,
my breasts like corners of a pillow,
and the children in the opposite row,
and their grandfather, all unclothed,
and so I pressed my eyelids closed,
but my hands faded to fans of bone
as I saw your womb full of shadow
scrabbled by a skeleton's embryo,
so I turned my face to the window
on a Saturday night over Glasgow
skulls thronging as light exploded
as black and white as ground zero
identity reduced to a puppet show
of fillings, piercings, the afterglow
of starlight flushing the world below
because it has nowhere else to go.

Eoghan Walls

THE RELIGIOUS IMPULSE IN A BUSTED FACE

We jump into the taxi and I shout, *Hospital!*
The baby bleeds on my shirt, her howls frantic,
and the heat rising off her scalp is phenomenal,

almost steaming from the activity of brain electrics
flashing and pulsing in the grey folds of her brain,
like storm clouds backlit by a turbulence of static.

I am trying to imagine the shape she gives her pain
like a Neanderthal clumsily composing a pantheon,
conjuring faces out of storm clouds over the plains

slouched, rocking a cub at the mouth of his den,
gibbering a hollow gospel of half-lipped syllables
as the deluge begins and passes and begins again.

Eoghan Walls

THE HORROR

Once surfaces were clear, and your own face
met you eye-to-eye from the mirror's centre
as you barefooted each room in three paces,
before your guts tore and you lost each other
to these soft-skinned emissions of your body,
riming your glassware with their fingerprints
and souring dairy products at your periphery
as they moan in a pidgin of misheard sentences;

until one night, groping bedwards from a piss,
she's there, your dead superimposed on her face,
muttering of how the life after yours is vicious
but certain; there is a catalogue of your mistakes
that will be replayed in worlds you do not own,
and it will matter what you have done, at home.

Jessica Traynor

ON SACKVILLE PLACE

From the cobbler's shop
I watch rain
paint the pavements brown.

A smell of sealant
and burnt metal
hangs below the strip-lights.

Outside, a man
with a thousand-yard stare
shouts *Johnno! Johnno! Johnno!*

An old woman
folds her umbrella,
says to the cobbler:

'When you think
of the grandchildren,
you wonder:

did I ever love
my own kids enough?'
Outside, buses snort,

puddles pucker, the click
of crutches keeps time
with the key-wheel as it spins.

The cobbler smiles
and shakes his head
'Ah no,' he says, 'ah no.'

Jessica Traynor

IKEA SLEEP
  *i.m. Peggy Mangan*

Miles of scrubland sub-dividing
sub-divided estates,
it's all distances here –

a long walk from Tuesday's crowds
to the blue, broken view
from the restaurant windows.

                ★


To wait with patience is a quality
shared by man, woman, dog,
as it is to fall out of memory,

to break through that
smoke-stack landscape,
get lost in its low-flying clouds.

                ★


Her shape was clear,
among the bushes,
once we got up close.

Catherine Phil MacCarthy

INVISIBLE GUESTS

Claire Dyer, *Eleven Rooms* (Two Rivers Press, 2013), £7.95.
Mary Turley-McGrath, *Forget The Lake* (Arlen House, 2014), €13.
Noel King, *The Stern Wave* (Salmon Poetry, 2013), €12.

In the title poem of Claire Dyer's eloquent first collection *Eleven Rooms*,
the speaker comments on a composition of Mondrian. Echoing Lewis
Carroll's Alice, she conjures accurately what it feels like to be human:

> I'm Alice, she says. Some days
> I can reach the walls. Others
> I'm a corner dot, so small the canvas
>
> could swallow me whole if it wished.

In Dyer's poems, the doors between memory, imagination and perception
open easily. Her observations are underpinned by a deep interiority, a
facility to move seamlessly between her external world and an inner one.
In 'Plunder', the speaker conjures a home that has been gutted:

> And I, who had no rights, crept in at night,
> a slipping-thief, soothed the *Danger* sign, *Keep Out!*,
> goat-scrambled in the street-lamp dark,
> unpicked from the rain what I could claim –
> my mother's smile, my dancing feet,
> walks with boys, hands in fallen leaves ...

Here, as in other poems, the language is highly textured and particular,
lines are woven into patterns, the rhythm of the voice appears effortless,
the imagery often laden with significance. Her surreal vision delivers a
vivid, intimate, sometimes erotic world of transition, and metamorphosis.
   In 'Ars Poetica?' Czesław Miłosz says:

> The purpose of poetry is to remind us
> how difficult it is to remain just one person,
> for our house is open, there are no keys in the doors,
> and invisible guests come in and out at will.

In Claire Dyer's poems, the guest may be a seal ('Visiting the Seals') or a
horse ('Talking to a Dead Horse') that the speaker identifies with before

she becomes transformed, in the space of a quiet line or two and a subtle shift of tone. Similarly, the woman who misses a last pre-dawn Jubilee Line train finds herself growing feather and wing, becomes gradually a bird, takes to the air and flies to Haarlem ('A Man with Pale Grey Eyes'). The houses, rooms, rivers, orchards that this poet inhabits, equally inhabit her, and the poems deliver a magical, dream-like clarity.

The title of Mary Turley-McGrath's second collection, *Forget the Lake*, prompts a question: *Why?* The title poem 'Lake Song' offers some clues, in answer to the refrain which begins each stanza: 'Sometimes I try to forget the lake, / to forget'. The speaker evokes the scene – 'that mile-long stretch of water overhung by woods' – in several moods. We are in no doubt about the beauty of the lake, its eeriness, suggested by the word 'caldera' in the first stanza, and the speaker's sense of dispossession in the second. And finally, the moon: 'A shaft of moonlight split / the room, reached the roses by my bed.' The violence is understated, but there all the same.

The poems in *Forget the Lake* are divided into four sections. The first two, 'Waterlines' and 'Land & Light', reflect a vivid sense of place, what Seamus Heaney has referred to as 'an imaginative nest', a beloved place that becomes a ground for the voice. There are lakes, rivers, fields, shore-lines, islands, strands, the sea. There's wonder in the everyday drama of weather, of waking to a mountain wrapped in mist, or a flooded field. Her lyrics often begin with moments of observation: 'The lake became an estuary overnight' ('Transitions'); or 'The moon over Rathlin / scans the Sea of Moyle' ('Rathlin'). The lines are rich in place names, whether of townland, locality, or field: Scribley Hill, Slough Field, Talbot's Castle, Roscarberry, Rathmullan, Cloonakellig.

What is conveyed here is a love of language, of the sounds of words in the mouth. Latin roots such as 'caldera', 'lunulae', 'abalone' and 'calends' speckle the lines. The imagery is startling, often sensual:

> ... That night I dreamt of sleeping
> in a summer meadow, my body covered with butterflies.
> — 'PEACOCK BUTTERFLY'

Or, 'Summer hesitates – just briefly – / like the missed breath of a sleeping child' ('The Change'); or, 'as midday sunlight is lanced by rain' ('Signs'). The third section, 'Silence with Words', reflects on the making of art, and on mortality. These poems are rich in travel references – Andalusia, Burma, Poland – and allusions to other cultures. 'Beginnings' is a sequence of seven poems that reflect on the birth of a firstborn child. Here, the distance between the speaker in the poem and author is less achieved, and the work more opaque as a result.

Mary Turley-McGrath's poems convey a sense of rootedness and ancestral connection, and also reflect the speaker's relation to the cosmos. 'Rathlin' ends: 'We slept / that night to the deep sea's moan, / so I felt I had been borrowed / by the sea, and returned home / with the morning sun.' In 'Surface', she writes of: 'how we can never be other than ourselves, / burning stars, disappearing into black holes'.

The title of Noel King's *The Stern Wave* comes from a line in the first poem in this, his second collection, titled 'Painter': 'I see ropes everywhere, am painting a series of knots: / love knots, / strangle knots, / a rolling hitch, / the Dutch cringle, / the slipper hitch, / the stern wave'. This collection includes fifty-nine poems on an eclectic range of topics, many written in the style of a dramatic monologue. Diverse personas are assumed: these are talky poems, mostly written in free verse, loosely structured. In 'Stilt School' the speaker is a Trinidadian teenager: 'My sneakers are super-glued man, / to planks of wood, long woods / so we can walk tall man, walk tall, / our teacher hav both feet on the earth'.

We hear a grandmother, a policeman, a domestic servant, schoolgirls, teenage boys, a migrant worker, and a tour guide in a poem titled 'Touring the Poet's House'. Several poems depict nightmare scenarios: 'He's twenty-eight, the mother's / out all day, he could be out all day; // but no, he pisses in the wash-hand basin, / never washes, his caveman hair falling over the cheeses // he scurries from the fridge / in the middle of the night' ('Grounded'). King's poems are full of people – comic, vulgar, sadistic, or suicidal: 'The mare is shooting shit / ahead of our headlights, / frantic this way that way' ('Black Horse'). Or they are detached, merciless observers: 'As your body / consecrated / itself on the steps / of a church altar, / she moved in agony / in the far field, / closing her eyes, / flinging / your dead baby in the bog' ('Ordination Day'). Several poems evoke premature death or suicide with tabloid efficiency: zany and grotesque, there is fascination and repulsion in equal measure.

Here and there, in 'Island', for instance, or 'The End of the Season', the poems become more mysterious as they move inward and reflect:

> row me to the mouth
> of the mountain river
>
> where the ancestors descended
> to our valley and settled
>
> row me like there is no tomorrow
>     – 'WHERE I COME FROM'

## Biddy Jenkinson

### V

Gan V a bheith san aibítir
níl samhailt litreach agam
dár lámha ag luascadh.
Ná níl litir agam don chruth
a dhéanann m'ordóg
agus mo mhéar thosaigh
agus mo smig anuas orthu
is mé ag machnav.

### CÚRAM SCRÍBHNEORA

A mhéarlorga a bhaint dá shaothar,
agus corrcheann a chur ar ais
d'fhonn dul amú
a chur ar léirmheastóirí.

### FÁINLEOGA SA GHRÉIG

Fáinleoga a tháinig isteach sa bhialann
trín doras,
a d'eitil chun na spéire istigh,
ceapadh iad
i gcruinneachán trédhearcach plaisteach na síleála
nach raibh oscailt air ná slí amach as.

Fir óga ghorma ina línte ar dhá thaobh na sráide
ag iarraidh málaí, uaireadóirí, dlúthdhioscaí a dhíol
le daoine
nach bhfuil málaí, uaireadóirí, dlúthdhioscaí uatha.

## Wendy Mooney

BUYING TIME

Because my mother said
*Go everywhere,*
*you never know who you'll meet*
I pause daytime television, numbed out,
cross the dual carriageway,

struck by a white car at Frascati –
as vivid as the bride in Venice
who stepped before me above the canal:

*Light-car full of airiness,*
*heaven car stop beside me –*

it passes, purrs on towards the Rock Road,
the back seat packed with darkness,
a fat man, bald and leaning forward
over the steering wheel.

To buy time before turning homeward
I trace the path for spilt coins –

a stub of orange crayon,
a dyed pink feather,
a set of discarded headphones –
two of my mother's grey hairs

on the cuff
of my unwashed hoodie
when I reach down to untangle them.

She's dead now.
Nobody calls these days.

# Mícheál Ó hAodha

Caitríona Ní Chléirchín, *An Bhrídeach Sí* (Coiscéim, 2014), €7.50.
Philip Cummings, *ad delectationem stultorum* (Coiscéim, 2012), €10.
Seán Ó Dúrois, *I nDán* (Coiscéim, 2013), €8.
Derry O'Sullivan, *Dúnann Dia a Dhoras Dé Domhnaigh* (Coiscéim, 2014), €7.50.
Marcus Mac Conghail, *Ceol Baile: dánta agus amhráin* (Coiscéim, 2014), €7.50.

It's not so long ago since some people were intimating that Irish-language poetry had become too urban and gimmicky. It was just a playground for middle-class *Gaeilgeoir*-type romantics who like to be viewed through the prism of various fashionable 'isms' – feminism, eco-criticism or whatever you're having yourself. Many of them were writers who secretly hankered after an audience for their work in translation (i.e., in English), or remained blinkered to the increased marginalisation and indeed disappearance of Irish as a community language, and its ongoing diminution in the official sphere, against a backdrop of increasing urbanisation. Or so the private 'script' went.

Anyone who picks up and reads any one of these five books would be disabused of this 'take' on poetry in the Irish language pretty quickly. Irish-language poets are breaking new ground and are more innovative (in many cases) than their peers writing in English. They are reviving old forms and experimenting with new ones on a constant basis, and even cross-fertilising art forms (poetry mixed with music and painting, along with new developments in the visual/acoustic spheres), while still remaining true to the essentials of the tradition.

We don't hear enough about female Irish-language poets in Ireland in general, the Westerners and Northerners in particular – Colette Ní Ghallchóir and Caitríona Ní Chléirchín, to mention just two examples of the latter. Ní Chléirchín is a very exciting talent as evidenced by her second volume, *An Bhrídeach Sí*, beautifully produced by Coiscéim. There is nothing 'gimmicky' about the love explored here; it is primeval and earthy and passionate; it is a struggle that takes an enormous toll on the lover. Ní Chléirchín rails against the prevailing zeitgeist by exploring love as a form of suffering, love as a lack of balance or an inequality. We live in the era of homogeneity and categorisation, where even feelings and rights can be weighed up and measured and assigned to their respective categories. There is no set of scales that can measure love or loss, however, as Ní Chléirchín reminds us. The poets of old, like the earliest philosophers, understood that suffering, despair and even hate are a constant aspect of the human condition. In Ní Chléirchín's finest poems, she draws on many older Gaelic tropes and reinvents them; she makes them new. In an inversion of the powerful *aisling* theme, Ní Chléirchín pictures the tormented woman of today awaiting redemption and release from the labyrinth of her emotions, personalised in the form of her male lover:

> fiochmhar an grá
> seachain seachain seachain
> — 'SÉALA'

Another poet who has remained true to the Gaelic tradition but who is moulding it and shaping it to suit a present-day sensibility is Belfast poet Philip Cummings, whose *ad delectationem stultorum* combines themes from Irish history and Gaelic culture with modern-day social commentary, often ironic or acerbic, in a way that is innovative and refreshing. Cummings has been one of Northern Ireland's Irish-language stalwarts over the years, and had a long association with Irish-language journalism in the troubled province. Particularly striking in this collection is his revival of the ancient tradition of proverbial triads, arguably one of the most strikingly original contributions to Irish-language writing in the current era. There is something magical about the way that Cummings links different eras and aspects of the Gaelic tradition and his own individual history with a modern sensibility, using irony and humour to do so. Unlike too many of his peers writing poetry in Irish today, Cummings knows when to apply the simple touch and the power of the short lyric. His best poems are these shorter lyrics, because, as with anything that reflects true beauty, they frequently echo something that is greater than itself:

> Trí fhocal lán draíochta:
> mo
> chéad
> rothar.

And:

> Trí S a thugann dearcadh nua:
> sliabh;
> sneachta;
> sliocht.

Another poet with a wonderful ability to capture the natural order of things and to mould them as art is Seán Ó Dúrois. Born in England, Ó

Dúrois has lived for many years in Belfast. He has won a number of Oireachtas na Gaeilge awards, including the main award for prose in 2001, and several awards for children's writing. He was the overall winner of the Strokestown Prize/Colmcille Prize in 2012 for his poem 'Dodekathlos', which is included in this collection of nearly 100 poems, entitled *I nDán*. With a knowledge of Japanese, Spanish and German, Ó Dúrois has contributed to the image of the modern Irish-language writer as an international figure. *I nDán* is a beautifully produced collection, published by Coiscéim, who previously and innovatively also published translations by Ó Dúrois of the stories of Japan's Ryūnosuke Akutagawa, generally regarded as the 'Father of the Japanese short story'. Like Cummings, Ó Dúrois has the range to make of myth – in his case, the parables and myths of ancient Greece – an exciting new impetus in Irish-language writing:

> Cá rachainn le hinspioráid a fháil?
> Níl tinfeadh le fáil a thuilleadh.
> Is fada an lá ó thuirling
> Teanga thine ar mo cheann.

> […]

> Tá gáire Thalia chomh géar le gloine bhriste
> Baineann sé macalla as na ballaí slíogairt
> Tá Melpomene ag caitheamh aníos sa chúinne,
> Tá Calliope ag fanacht le laoch.
>
> – 'INSPIORÁID'

There are few enough poets in any language whose writing gets better with age, but Derry O'Sullivan, now in his early seventies, is definitely one of them. In 2012 a translation of his 'Marbhghin 1943: Glaoch ar Liombó' was awarded the prestigious *The Times* Stephen Spender Prize. One of his major themes in *Dúnann Dia a Dhoras Dé Domhnaigh*, other than his superb meditations on Paris – his home-in-exile and a city he has lived in for many decades – is the ancient Gaelic love for place as transposed to the betwixt-and-between sensibility of the modern-day poet. Masterful in his handling of imagery, particularly the new-born image that catches his reader unawares, O'Sullivan's poetry is nearly too rich at times – if such is possible – like the bough of a tree heavily laden with fruit. His images of Paris by night, a city furled into itself and in need of coaxing, are like small paintings, wonderful and surprising at the same time:

Gráinneog í an chathair anocht
A dheineann ceirtlín di féin,
Cuachta i bpóca na hoíche

[…]

Caithim catsúil ar a hata gealaí
Is gléasaim mo chosa i mbróga tairní.
                    – 'PÁRAS ISTOÍCHE'

O'Sullivan's poems have a wonderful visual power, whereas Marcus Mac Conghail's first collection, *Ceol Baile: dánta agus amhráin*, heralds an exciting new voice that celebrates music and indeed the music that is poetry. Mac Conghail is still finding his voice, but he has already moored himself at the original berth that was the function of poetry for centuries. After all, the Gaelic poets of the past frequently recited and sang their poetry to musical accompaniment. Mac Conghail mixes the personal with the universal, and as the father of a young family myself, I like the way he transforms the everyday struggles of family life into poetry.

Mac Conghail's songs and lyrical poetry explore both love and death and the lives of other poets and musicians at a local and universal level. And as with many of the best poets, it is the simplest lyrics that frequently carry the most power:

Leoithne bhog ghaoithe
ag cigilt ceoil
as sreang ghiotáir
le séideadh an chuirtín
– 'SEOMRA SAMHRAIDH'

Proinsias Ó Drisceoil

BLESSING OF THE SPIRIT

Somhairle MacGill-Eain, *Ó Choill go Barr Ghéaráin: Na Dánta*, maille le haistriúcháin Ghaeilge le Paddy Bushe (Coiscéim, 2013), €20.
Maoilios Caimbeul, *Tro Chloich na Sùla: Mar a Chunnaic Peantairean Ainmeil an Saoghal* (Clàr, 2014), £9.99.

Scottish and Irish Gaelic derive from a shared root, but long centuries of separate development mean that they may now be regarded as distinct languages, although enjoying a fair amount of mutual comprehension, particularly in their written forms. Analogies with say, Galician, Portuguese and Spanish or Czech and Slovak suggest themselves and as with these, it is the narcissisms of minor difference rather than more obvious dissimilarities that can pose difficulty for translators.

Sorley MacLean / Somhairle MacGill-Eain (1911–1996) is the only Scottish Gaelic poet with an international reputation: his influence on those who have followed him as poets in that language is unsurpassed. His vocabulary and metrical technique are complex, difficult to re-present and this, allied to his reputation, makes translation problematic. Gaelic did not come under a sustained modernisation impulse like that experienced by the major languages but it has profound expressive possibilities and these allowed MacLean to eschew neologism while plumbing the language's entire range, not least the use of abstract forms of the language with which preachers on his native Raasay – home of the Free Presbyterian church – had familiarised him. MacLean translated virtually all of his poems into English, but claimed that the English versions were mere cribs; however, their source gives these versions an authority which it is difficult for an English-language translator to challenge. MacLean was a Symbolist modernist, but one who combined this with obscure allusion to the Gaelic tradition in poetry, history and politics; this can create difficulties for readers and translators, something the volume under review has sought to alleviate by including a brief guide to the more arcane references.

Paddy Bushe comes to the task of translating MacLean with the credentials of an established poet in Irish and the over-riding intention is to render valid poems in Irish, an ambition which he successfully manages to realise. Internal rhyme drives many MacLean poems and Bushe maintains this technical prowess, rhyming, for example, 'mórgachta' and 'Beethoven' in line with MacLean's long 'o' rhyming of 'mòrachd' and 'Beethoven' ('Cochur'), to mention a particularly exotic example.

The very title of the book under review proclaims the difficulties facing the translator. *O Choille gu Bearradh* was published as MacLean's collected poems in 1989, and this collection in its entirety comprises the present volume. However the word 'bearradh' (ridge) is not common in Irish and 'droim', the obvious Irish equivalent, is ambiguous in also meaning 'back' in the sense of 'posterior'. Bushe translates it as 'barr ghéaráin', not a readily understood form but one which apparently occurs as a placename on Mount Brandon in Kerry. Similar issues abound – an Irish equivalent for the word 'sgùrr' ('high, sharp-pointed hill') failed to materialise and Bushe leaves it in its Scottish form, a tribute to the more mountainous landscape which underlies Scottish Gaelic topographical vocabulary.

*O Choille gu Bearradh* was published in 1989 with many typos and textual flaws, some of which were rectified in a subsequent edition. The appearance of the definitive *Collected Poems* of MacLean in 2011 marginalised the 1989 collection and the editors, Christopher Whyte and Emma Dymock, included personally sensitive poems that MacLean had not wished to have included in *O Choille gu Bearradh*. The latter work has had its relevance further diminished by the reform of Gaelic spelling in 2005, something fully embraced in the 2011 volume.

Bushe has, however, stayed with the forms of the 1989 edition and has printed the Scottish and Irish versions on facing pages. Much of what purports to be poetic translation in English generally is done in blissful ignorance of source languages, but this is not the case here: full account is taken of the originals, in particular of their rhythm, stylistic devices and spirit. MacLean's gift was for the lyric, but he wrote two very long sustained poems: these, 'An Cuilithionn' ('The Cuillin') and 'Coillte Rathasair' ('The Woods of Raasay'), are translated by Bushe without loss of either pace or form, a considerable achievement given the resonance and referential scale of the originals, let alone the labour involved:

> Tha mi cràiteach mun each bhuadhar
> a thogadh a cheann àrd thar chuantan,
> a bheireadh an dùbhlan le shèitrich
> do ghailebheinn a' Chuain Shiair ag èirigh.
>      – 'AN CUILITHIONN', PART 3

> (I am pained for the victor horse
> that would lift his high head over the seas,
> that would challenge with his neighing
> the mountainous surge of the western ocean rising)

In Irish this becomes:

Tá mé cráite faoin gcapall buamhar
ar ardaíodh a cheann thar farraigí móra,
a thabharfadh dúshlán lena chuid seitrigh
do ghal-bheanna na mara thiar suaite.

Translators are necessarily also interpreters and translation can easily
stray into explanation, a tendency from which these translations are not
exempt. The first verse of MacLean's early poem "A Chiall 's a Ghràidh"
('Reason and Love') is:

Ma thubhairt ar cainnt gu bheil a' chiall
co-ionann ris a' ghaol,
chan fhior dhi.

(If our language has said that reason
is identical with love
it is not speaking the truth)

Bushe translates this as:

Má dúirt ár dteanga go bhfuil gaol
idir na focail ar *grá* is ar *ciall*
ní fíor di.

This translation plays cleverly on the word 'gaol' – 'love' in Scotland,
'relationship, connection' in Ireland – but the verse as translated is,
perhaps unavoidably, more exegesis than translation.

However, Irish now has a definitive and highly readable version of the
MacLean *oeuvre*, and the book comes with a brief foreword translated
from Seamus Heaney, and with an essay by Breandán Ó Doibhlin which
summarises MacLean's achievement as effectively as one would expect
from one who has written authoritatively on MacLean over many
decades.

Recent re-editing by Christopher Whyte of the MacLean poems is
subjected to challenge in *Tro Chloich na Sùla*, the most recent collection
from an eminent legatee of MacLean, the Skye poet Maoilios Caimbeul/
Myles Campbell. In a note which accompanies the collection he objects
to MacLean's lines from 'Ùrnaigh' ...

A chionn nach eil dìon ann
agus a chionn nach eil m' iarrtas
ach 'na fhaileas faoin sgeulachd

(Because there is no refuge
and because my desire
is only the vain reflection of a story)

... being changed to the anti-Christian:

A chionn nach eil Dia ann
agus a chionn nach eil Crìosda
ach 'na fhaileas faoin sgeulachd

(Since there is no God
And since Christ
Is only the vain reflection of a story )

MacLean had published the less controversial (and less intelligible) version in *O Choille gu Bearradh* in order to save his mother from upset, but in Campbell's view Whyte was not entitled to make the substitution even though research showed that these were MacLean's original lines. Campbell is the joint author of the autobiographical *Island Conversion: The Transition of a Gaelic Poet from Sceptic to Believer* (2011), and the collection under review is unusual in including 'An Cruthaighear' (the creator) among those thanked, so it can reasonably be assumed that the objection is on grounds of faith. In his response, 'Ùrnaigh Eile', Campbell makes a statement of his religious beliefs and characterises the issues at the heart of this disagreement as a deliberation between Athens and Jerusalem in which the latter will be vindicated:

Bidh Ierusalem ag ùrnaigh
's an Àithne ri fanaid
gus an tig a'mhadainn ùr ud –
's nèamh is talamh air an ceangal.
                    –'ÙRNAIGH EILE'

(Jerusalem will be praying
and Athens be poking fun
until that new morning comes
and earth and heaven are connected)

*Tro Chloich na Sùla* ('Through the Ball of the Eye') derives its title from an extended series of poems which offer homage to outstanding works of visual art beginning with Leonardo da Vinci's painting, 'The Virgin of the Rocks', and ending with 'Nighthawks' by Edward Hopper. The poems in the series are written in slightly informal versions of *dán díreach*, the metres employed in the encomia perfected by the medieval Gaelic poets, thus allowing high art poetry to express reverence for the high art of the painter. Colour has a moral purpose:

> Mura h-eil na dathan dorch'
> Ag innleachd am maoidheadh fhèin
>   – 'SEABHAGAN OIDHCHE (1942) / EDWARD HOPPER'

> (If the dark colours
> are not devising their own threat)

The *ùmhlachd* or humility essential to the artist is vital to salvation:

> Mur coimhead e suas le ùmhlachd
> Chan fhaigh e 'rìoghachd no tròcair.
>   – 'NEBUCHADNEZZAR (1795) / UILLEAM BLAKE'

> (If he does not look up with humility
> he will not obtain the kingdom or mercy)

Painting represents the possibility of moving beyond 'wilderness and copulation and the mysteriousness of greed' – "fàs / Is feis' is dìomhaireachd sannt", from 'Dannsa na Beatha (1899–1900)', after Edvard Munch. Each poem moves in its final verse towards the creative power of redemption. Thus Gauguin's 'Vision after the Sermon' is:

> A' guidhe beannachd an Spioraid,
> Is gum bi iad uile slàn.
>   – 'AISLING ÀS DÈIDH AN T-SEARMOIN (1888)'

> (Wishing for the blessing of the spirit,
> and that they may all be whole)

These are poems of craft and intelligence. *Tro Chloich na Sùla* is in Gaelic only: the Campbell cribs are by the reviewer; the English versions of Sorley MacLean are by the poet himself.

Liam Ryan

THE MEADOW
   *after Czesław Miłosz*

It's more than enough now
after more than forty years,
to chance on the smell of hay
for the satchels of memory to burst
and feel again the fork in my hands,
the welts across my palms,
see the swathes bristling
dust dancing in the sunlight,
hear the guttural accents
arguing about hurling matches,
hear father tracing and teasing,
smell the whiff of the Gold Flakes,
the yellow box in the stubble.

But there is no going back
that field is poached and pockmarked,
the hedges and ditches overgrown,
the trees cut for firewood;
the matches fought and forgotten,
all of the men dead and buried,
lost to us forever, forever.
This life is not some trial run,
regardless of our misunderstandings.
Can I instead find the courage
to follow the rhythm of my breath,
can I turn within, can I trust,
can I reap the harvest of this meadow?

# Edward Doegar

TWO KUṚIÑCI VERSES

Because you never wanted to cup your hands here
and swallow this peat-rinsed heathery water
and let it spill over your chin and under your shirt;
because you never felt thirsty, felt your tongue dry
and your lips turn tender, because you never knelt,
because you never wanted to, can I trust you?

★

After a little Spring rain the hillside opens its palms,
leaves bloated with green. We muddy our sandals here
where the path is a gushing riverbed. Monkeys jump
between branches, landing with a patter of applause.
We wander through the ruined tea set of a magnolia,
together we pour them out, the last few cups, one by one.

Jocelyn Page

EVERY SO OFTEN, A LETTER

He skims the opening about the weather, Pa's back, the freemartin
    born in May,
and slows at first mention of Joy – her first steps chasing a pair
    of Monarchs

across the reservoir's bad-luck meadow, her habit of waking in
    the night,
scared to pieces of the moon's sometimes blink, sometimes
    unstoppable eye.

No mention of Caroline herself; no heart, no arms or lips, only
    a glimpse
of her fingers busy sewing quilts, stewing tomatoes, making
    dandelion tiaras

to balance on Joy's curls as she totters and trips through fields.
    He leans
against the general store's doorframe in that one long strip of
    a town

and searches the road from where he came, to where he's going,
    and then
for someone to pick on, or pity, for any old symbol or sign.

Jocelyn Page

HE GATHERED THINGS FROM THE BLACK HILLS' TRAIL

Things he could imagine back at the house, on the kitchen table,
    the windowsill: a scarlet
tanager's feather, the wilted trumpet of a mimbre blossom, a
    beavertail cactus paddle,

separated,
            flowerless and bristled, limp yet heavy, oozing where it
had broken from the plant.
Like this, on a steep descent in Wyoming, he chose presents for her
    second birthday.

David Wheatley

## FOG, CAFÉS AND BEDROOMS

Rosemary Tonks, *Bedouin of the London Evening: Collected Poems* (Bloodaxe Books, 2014), £12.
Peter Manson, *Poems of Frank Rupture* (Sancho Panza, 2014), £8.

Among the first things you spot are the dashes, ellipses and exclamation marks. Others may prefer their poems to come with a more ... unruffled surface, but – not Rosemary Tonks! It's a second-hand French thing. Of public transport in Kurdistan: 'The trains come in, boiling, caked!' Must she say goodbye alone? 'No one to see me off – Ah!' The horror of it all, 'the same flow of gutter-sugar to the brain ...' Never mind seeing her off, what about the welcome home party? It's long overdue: almost forty years, by my reckoning. Rosemary Tonks was born in 1928 and died as a writer, sensationally, sometime in the 1970s, only resurfacing now after her actual death in April 2014. Some lucky souls will have had the original volumes all along, but most of us have had to love her 'from the day she died', in Michael Hartnett's words for his grandmother. She is the great *symboliste* might-have-been of post-war British poetry, author of spectral lyrics Prufrock could have taken to heart, fond as they are 'of nocturnal strolls / And the immortal dirt of London / Under the clear panes of its nails'.

*Bedouin of the London Evening* comprises two collections, *Notes on Cafés and Bedrooms* and *Iliad of Broken Sentences*. Subtract the fog, the cafés and bedrooms and almost nothing remains, but what fog, cafés and bedrooms! The fog lies like a fire-blanket over everything, stifling all willpower and mutterings from Valéryan heretics that *'Il faut tenter de vivre'*:

> It's the café and the boredom, in the semi-dark
> People have a certain rank elegance
> And the dirt-encrusted street with its great jar of water
> Keeps my blood too fresh and truculent for work.

On occasion, sex is had ('We set about acquiring one another / Urgently!'), but the sequel is rarely satisfying: 'Criminal, I damn you for it (very softly)'. She circulates through London like her titular Bedouin, preening herself 'on the advantage of being ill-treated by the World' and indulging a Rimbaldian relish for the words 'bestial' and 'atrocious'.

Nor do the affinities with *le divin enfant* stop there. For many readers, Tonks's appeal is closely tied up with her disappearance after her collapse into religious mania. In her paranoia, she destroyed a collection of Asian art described as 'priceless' in Neil Astley's introduction, while his attempts to enter into communication with her are the subject of much *Aspern Papers*-like farce ('postcard from Satan', reads a diary entry prompted by the receipt of an Astley postcard). Tonks was not quite the recluse of popular myth after her abandonment of poetry: she, or Mrs Lightband (her born-again name), still loved cafés and was an *habituée* of Speaker's Corner. The small print in the footnotes reveals the existence of over a hundred post-poetic notebooks, presumably full of religious ramblings, and now in the University of Exeter archive, if anyone is interested. I wonder, though, whether there isn't something unsavoury about our interest in Tonks as a vanished poet. Most poets vanish sooner or later via the time-honoured route of no one wanting to publish or read them, so the thought of a poet, any poet, actively repelling our interest cannot help but seem freakish. Perhaps this says more about us than it does about Tonks.

A serious point to be made about her disappearing act is how close the poems seem, at any given moment, to darting out of the room. She is Gallic to the point of self-parody, but just as Rimbaud's drunken boat (in Beckett's translation) 'want[ed] none of Europe's waters', Tonks too wants out: 'the whole of Europe [...] is not enough'. It took Barbara Everett to wake people up to Larkin's French symbolist side, with those 'Immensements!' in 'Sad Steps' and his self-description as the 'Laforgue of Pearson Park'. Maybe he got it from Tonks (he includes her in his *Oxford Book of Twentieth-Century English Verse*), and maybe she is the source for the Laforguian percolations visible in early Sean O'Brien too. To a reader fresh from this book the 1960s will never look the same again: versions of literary history then and now that omit her will seem specious and threadbare. It's early days in the reabsorption of Tonks's work, but 'Poet and Iceberg', 'The Sofas, Fogs, and Cinemas', 'Addiction to an Old Mattress' and 'Song of the October Wind' are breath-catching poems. But really, why stop there? Swallow her whole. 'Oh yes, it's atrocious', as she says in 'Students in Bertorelli's': 'Certainly it's literature.'

The case of Peter Manson provides another handy example of canonical speciousness. Born in 1969, Manson should be as well-known as Paul Farley or Nick Laird, but the career openings for Mallarmé translators of known deviant tendencies are not what they might be. Fans of Eric Idle's post-*Python* vehicle, *Rutland Weekend Television*, may remember a wonderful gibberish-based chat show whose host welcomes viewers with the words 'Ham sandwich, bucket and water plastic

Duralex rubber McFisheries underwear'; Manson is to your average slim volume what Rutland Weekend Television is to Channel 4 News. In 'Fragments of a Narcissus' he shows himself a dab hand at nonsense poetry, with a delivery reminiscent of William Empson's 'steady iron-hard jet of absolutely total nonsense, as if under great pressure from a hose'. A grounding in Tom Raworth might be of help for the uninitiated (Sancho Panza also publish Raworth's *XIV Liners*). Reading the long central sequence, 'Sourdough Mutation', I was strongly reminded of Christian Bök's *Eunoia* and its paronomasiac free-for-all. What on earth is going on here, you think, before the eye adjusts to the patterns and it all makes – I nearly said 'sense'. Manson performs deft little acts of boustrophedon, ploughing his words back into themselves in reverse:

> no gendered
> endearment
>
> a mentor
> to torment
>
> all meant as
> amen

For 'aphorist fog hat' read 'a fat forest hog'. If we can live with this kind of thing coming from Paul Muldoon, it shouldn't be so much of a stretch to extend the same courtesy to Manson. But since this kind of writing does, it's fair to say, generate some resistance, I'd like to suggest a musical analogy. Manson's reversible word-cells are like Webern's tone-rows. Just as the Austrian used his tone-rows to go beyond diatonic melody, Manson uses his wordplay to push language beyond the plausible concatenations of conventional narrative. If Webern sounds a bit severe, other points of reference might include Kurtág or the Ligeti of the *Nonsense Madrigals* – avant-garde composers who are, first and last, tremendous *fun*. 'Pleasure is all', as Manson says, and as Wallace Stevens insisted too, in 'Notes Toward a Supreme Fiction' ('It must give pleasure').

It comes with a strong political flavour too. So many discussions of political poetry fixate on content, as though content is ever separable from form, but among Manson's achievements – and 'Fragments of a Narcissus' seems to me political poetry of a high order – is to have found a way of redirecting the violence done to language by a broken politics back whence it came. If 'unobtainium munition dumps', 'burst non-dom subliminal threshing floor shingled' and 'autopsy powerless collagen agenda armature manure' aren't rolling news headlines on Murdoch channels just yet, they will be, soon.

Manson's versions of Mallarmé, *The Poems in Verse*, are among the best translations of our time, and with luck at least some readers will think *Poems of Frank Rupture* are an attempt to render this Frank Rupture bloke into English. A foreign poet who definitely exists is Baudelaire, whose portrait by Nadar scowls beatifically from Manson's cover, but who doesn't feature anywhere in the book. He doesn't need to, since he and his *confrères* are everywhere in Manson, Holy Spirit-like. John Ashbery and Ciaran Carson have been rightly hailed for their versions of Rimbaud, but when it comes to making the heroic French nineteenth century new, this is how it's done and no mistake. If we expect our poets to write out of an experientially defined self, to 'find their voice', and take the assault course of form by cranking out the odd villanelle, then Manson can only baffle and disappoint. Expecting him to do these things, however, I would suggest, is no more meaningful than expecting Webern to write 'Yankee Doodle Dandy'. Equally wrong-headed would be the suggestion that this kind of thing had its chance back in the day and failed to stick. No less than Bök's *Eunoia*, this poetry is thrillingly of the present moment, and pregnant with possibility for anyone who cares to absorb it. I have seen the future and it (still) works. Or, as BBC's 1970s sketch show, *Rutland Weekend Television*, might and in fact did put it: 'Rustically inclined? Of course. Sick in a cup, successfully douched dinner bottom, whenever cobbled therein.'

Miriam Gamble

## BOUNDARIES UNDRAWN

Zoë Skoulding, *The Museum of Disappearing Sounds* (Seren Books, 2013), £8.99.
Pascale Petit, *Fauverie* (Seren Books, 2014), £9.99.
Kerry Hardie, *The Zebra Stood in the Night* (Bloodaxe Books, 2014), £9.95.

In 'Metamorphic', Zoë Skoulding writes that 'What's / unintelligible isn't silent, isn't transcendent / blank: it's most of it, including you'. Unintelligibility is to the fore in *The Museum of Disappearing Sounds*: this is consciously experimental work which proceeds largely without punctuation or even the assistance that, in punctuation's absence, carefully chosen line breaks can provide. Indeed, Skoulding's poems actively fray such structural guide-ropes: the line breaks have been chosen carefully, but they've been chosen to flout rather than aid any effort to construe an ongoing line of thought.

In 'Room 401', part of a sequence of 'room' poems which conclude the book, she observes that 'the / beginning of the sentence slips away / before you reach the end'; in 'Room 127', she writes of 'voices / uninterruptedly saying nothing'. These rooms are at least partially identified with poetry (the room of the stanza), and it's presented by them as a language mechanism which, however battled against, will ultimately trump individual efforts at expression:

> I'm just playback
>       all pauses and stutters
> smoothed out in the dimensions of a room

Beckett's trilogy can be discerned in the background here, as can Orwell's warnings about the 'ready-made phrases' endemic to political writing. If Skoulding's work tasks its reader, it does so with the intention of revealing both how slipshod our conceptions of self are and how readily language is used upon us as a sedative, or as an active agent of delusion. In 'television',

> history flutters under
> our eyelids in sleeping screens
> events take place or tàke the
> place of events

In 'Gropers', a now-extinct criminal slang is revived with the suggestion that sub-languages secretly surround us, mouthing dark truths. Both world and self are incorrigibly plural in these poems, though sometimes most vividly so at the level of idea.

Many of the poems in Pascale Petit's *Fauverie* enlist animals as a means of confronting the trauma of parental abuse, and the book tracks a process of attempted healing through this ongoing act of imaginative reconstitution. Although occasionally the parallels are starkly direct (in 'Blackbird', for example, where 'the darkness / sang // through the keyhole / of my yellow beak'), many of the animal-human conjunctions are bizarre: 'Your Letter is a Przewalski Horse'; 'My Mother's Salmon Skin Nightdress'. In the latter poem, we see the child Petit sewing her mother's nightgown:

> All my childhood I sew, mending it until bedtime
> and each morning it's in tatters.

The animal analogies work in a similar fashion: they communicate themselves as continuing and strained attempts to understand, and to resolve through neo-mythic reconfiguration. The stitches are meant to show – both because the effort of reshaping this material is unutterably difficult, and because the poet's art is her strength – her potential salvation. It's only through artistry that she can rework her world as she needs to in order to survive, to triumph over experience; therefore it is on full display and its non-realism is actively celebrated.

Paris, the city of Petit's birth, is for the bulk of the book the father's terrain: he absorbs it into himself, consumes and embodies it; on his deathbed, 'All of Paris is quiet, while the oxygen machine / struggles to fill [his] lungs' ('My Father's City'). It's not his actual death which enables Petit to forge a changed relation to the city, but her repeated reconsideration of that death in poetry; ultimately, this re-seeing is what makes her strong enough to 'pluck / her father's city out of the drains / and hold it up for the sun's inspection' ('Resurrection'). Beneath its colourful panache, this is darkly urgent writing in which Petit works through unfinished business with the 'cellar "me"' the poems seek to release:

> She is the silence.
> I am the scream.
>         – 'CELLAR'

Kerry Hardie's poetry is quieter in its approach, though no less concerned with the necessity for self-tutelage and self-development. In *The Zebra Stood in the Night* she too finds existing models wanting: in the prose poem 'The Conjurer', she speaks of being 'tired of poems – their carefulness, their form and rhyme and crafted double meanings', and in 'Nobby of the Bogs' she turns what begins as a recognisable lyric format (meditation on the pregnant moment of perception) upside down, switching the focus from what's been seen onto all that's missed:

> Seeing the heron
> was seeing
> the knowing that it happens
> whether we see it or not.

Again, in 'Caherdaniel', the self stands within the landscape's 'circle of attention', not the other way round. World and self are in constant exchange in part one of *The Zebra Stood in the Night*: in 'Washing', 'the way we live' is exposed to external view, while 'wind and rain and lit weather' enter the domestic space; in 'Reflection', 'The terrain external' explicitly 'mirrors the terrain internal' – as swallows skim 'the face of the rushy meadow', thoughts break 'the line of the line of light'.

These are not simplistic parallels, or parallels remarked simply for the sake of remarking them. Part two of the collection opens with an essay on grief, followed by a series of poems all but one of which are addressed to Hardie's brother, who died in 2012. Despite its frequent zest for phenomena ('I think we are "saved" back into life by matter', she says in 'Aftermath'), part one is equally coloured by loss. Like Petit, Hardie is formulating a new way of seeing in the poems; through them, she is teaching herself to let go 'the urge for ordering' that will implode in the face of what cannot be changed, cannot be bent to our desires. For a poet, this also involves rethinking the way in which the poem broaches the world. Hardie's skills as a lyric poet are second to none (particularly, she is a mistress of the short, complex but simply expressed poem, as in 'Song', 'Washing', 'Poplars' and 'Child'), and the meeting of that ability with the need to break new ground is productive of exceptional writing, reminiscent but by no means derivative of Elizabeth Bishop in its combination of attention to detail and startling, subtly worked-towards insight.

Leontia Flynn

THE RADIO

The radio hoots and mutters, hoots and mutters
out of the dark, each morning of my childhood.
A kind of plaintive, reedy, oboe note –
*Deadlock* ... it mutters, *firearms* ... *Sunningdale;*
*Just before two this morning* ... *talks between* ...

and through its aperture, the outside world
comes streaming, like a magic lantern show,
into our bewildered solitude.
*Unrest* ... it hoots now *both sides* ... *sources say* ...
My mother stands, like a sentinel, by the sink.

★

I should probably tell you more about my mother:
Sixth child of twelve surviving – 'escapee'
from the half-ignited *powder keg* of Belfast;
from its *escalation*, its *tensions ratcheting*
its *fear of reprisals*, and its *tit-for-tat.*

She is small, freaked out, pragmatic, vigilant;
she's high-pitched and steely   like, in human form,
The RKO transmitter tower, glimpsed
just before films on Sunday afternoons,
where we loaf on poufs – or wet bank holidays.

Or perhaps a strangely tiny lightning rod
snatching the high and wild and worrying words
out of the air, then running them to ground.
My mother sighs and glances briefly round
at her five small children. *How* does she have five kids?

★

Since my mother fell on the Wheel Of Motherhood
– that drags her, gasping, out of bed each dawn
bound to its form – she's had to rally back.
She wrangles her youngsters into one bright room
and tries to resist their centrifugal force

as she tries to resist the harrowing radio,
with its *Diplock* ... and *burned out* ... and *Disappeared*.
So high, obscure and far from neighbouring farms
is the marvellous bungalow my father built,
birdsong and dog-barks ricochet for miles;

and wasn't my mother wise to stay put here
soothed by the rhythms of a *culchie* Life
– birdsong in chimneys, the Shhhh of coal-truck brakes –
when women at home are queuing round the block
for their '*Valium, thank you doctor, and Librium*'?


*

So daily the radio drops its explosive news
and daily my mother turns to field the blow.
The words fall down, a little neutral now,
onto the stone-cold, cold, stone kitchen floor.
Our boiler slowly digests its anthracite

and somewhere outside, in the navy dark,
my father tends to his herd of unlikely cows.
A *Charolais*, the colour of cement,
thought to be lost for days has just turned up
simply standing – *ta da!*– in front of a concrete wall.

My mother, I think, is like that *Charolais* cow
in the Ulster of 1970 ... 80 ...what?
with its *tensions* ... and its *local sympathies*.
She gets her head down, hidden in plain view,
and keeps us close. '*Look: Nothing to see here – right?*'


*

But when the night has rolled round again,
my mother will lie unsleeping in her bed;
she'll lie unsleeping in that bungalow bed
and if a car slows on the bend behind the house,
she's up, alert – fearing the worst, which is:

that a child of hers might die – or lose an eye;
or a child *anywhere* die or lose an eye …
That the car which slows on the bend behind the house
– *Midnight* … she thinks now … *random* … *father of five* –
is the agent of vile sectarian attack.

By the top field's wall, our unfenced slurry pit,
(villain of Public Information Films)
widens and gulps beneath the brittle stars.
My mother too thinks the worst, then gulps it back,
and in this way discovers equilibrium.

\*

Death in the slurry pit, death beside the curb.
Death on the doorstep, bright-eyed, breathing hard.
My mother folds the tender, wobbling limbs
and outsized heads of her infants into herself;
she curls up, foetal, over our foetal forms.

Since my mother sailed down the Mekong river at nightfall
to the Heart of Darkness that is motherhood,
her mind's been an assemblage of wounds.
She thinks about Gerard McKinney, Jean McConville
– later the eyes of Madeleine McCann

will level their gaze from every pleading poster
and pierce her heart like a rapier – needle-thin
as the high, wild, hardly audible cries of children.
*Men of Violence* … says the radio.
My mother nods, then finally falls asleep.

\*

And what if after my mother falls asleep
the hoots, half-words, and notes of high alarm
get loose from her head on little soot-soft wings?
Say they flap like bats. They fuck with the carriage clock.
They settle on her Hummel figurines.

Till the whole contraption of that home-made house
creaks, roars and bulges with the soundless strain
of my mother trying not to be afraid ...
*Forgive me, this is all hypothesis.*
*It's conjecture, Doctor, of the crudest sort ...*

Its gist being: beneath our bonhomie
and tight commercial smiles, this tone or timbre
flows on, like a circuit thrown into reverse –
and at the centre of concentric circles
that this is what plays behind an unmarked door.

★

Sometimes, rather, lying in my bed
I seem to hear the sound of the radio
issuing from a room, deep in the house;
it tells, in mournful tones, how two young men
were *taken from their car beside the road ...*

and afterwards ... nothing. All the stars come out
like sparkling glitter in a magic globe
that ends beyond the dunes fringing the fields –
and because I'm still a child and understand
nothing at all, I simply fall asleep.

## John Sewell

ONE DAY
  *– in memory of Ann Atkinson*

The blackbird is singing by the room you woke in;
same split oak whistling in the range at breakfast, though the air
outside is warm. The lake too. Remember wading in
it seemed forever, through the slatey shallows of the bay;
that wind-shored hike onto High Spy; the meal you served
that evening; an after-life of poems shared.

At the time, one day among many, replayable surely
as and when? The blackbird after all is back again
on the lilac, this time singing everyone to sleep
and you – with such an eagerness – into our waking.

Richard Lambert

SNOW AT THE WINDOW

The snow seems like something a man mid-stumble
bearing a box of shell and stone

might fling, making suddenly unknown
where any stone or shell might go

and trying, even now, mid-fall, to fumble
each spinning flake of white, each pale tone,

back into its box, the way that I disown,
or try to, everything but snow at the window.

Richard Lambert

TO THE MOON

It's true that the hedgehog is bundled in leaves
    and the swans have flown over the water.
You're faint as a glimmering stone in the stream
    or the scar on a friend's lovely arm;
you've gone all the way to the end of the sky –
    when are you coming home?

Andrew Deloss Eaton

THE PHILOSOPHER

  A stone hides
at the bottom of a pond
when the pond is disturbed.
A cobblestone's curve fits
in the space of an empty palm.
Wet in lamplight it gives off lamplight.
Dry in daylight it is like a stone
at the bottom of a clear pond.
At the bottom of a muddy pond is a stone.
The curve of a cobblestone
and what I want to say is like that now
   when I imagine it.

Andrew Deloss Eaton

MEN IN WATER

i.
I know a man can feel at home at sea.

But on the sea, in it two full nights
hanging like a buoy above the deep
is a new story, the scene a parable.
We learn the way a single body drifts
from its ring of others gathered round
the raft, the cold rubber. The quiet

laps against us, the cold moon's teeth.


ii.
Of course, I did not notice then
but you will have seen those photographs
of people wearing coloured suits in air

falling from a plane, holding hands,
a halo bound for earth – it was like that
without the suits, the thrill.

Maria Johnston

UNDERSTANDABLE AND STILL UNGRASPABLE

Geoffrey Hill, *Broken Hierarchies: Poems 1952 – 2012*, edited by Kenneth Haynes (Oxford University Press, 2013), hb £45.

While carrying out research in Ireland's National Library some months ago, I was intrigued to discover a fan letter from a young Michael Longley to Geoffrey Hill, dating from 1971. 'Just a short note to say how very impressed I am by *Mercian Hymns*', Longley enthused: 'A copy eventually filtered through to Belfast and I've read it several times with increasing pleasure.' Longley would go on to publicly praise Hill's 'profound genius' as a maker of 'exquisite, immaculate music', but what strikes one most of all in this private communication is the image presented of the ordinary life that is trying to go on amid the intensifying violence of the Troubles. 'We paddle along between bullets and explosions and manage to cultivate our little back gardens', Longley described the day-to-day scene, and it is an image of keeping going, of the imperative to cultivate critical and creative vitality in the face of sterility and enervation. For me, the snapshot of Longley sitting in conflict-torn Belfast reading again and again Hill's enchanting, earth-shattering sequence puts the focus not only on the very special pressures that are placed on the poet in such anarchic times and on how poetry may be 'a sad and angry / consolation', but also on the figure of the reader him / herself. How can the reader hope to match the poet's energy and meet the considerable challenge of such poetry when quotidian life with its own consuming activities, major or minor, cannot but intervene?

Such a question was brought home to me in an immediate way when I found myself struggling to review *Broken Hierarchies* – all 940 pages of it – in the weeks after giving birth to my first child. Physically and mentally exhausted, the task of holding in hand, never mind reading and responding to, this colossal volume was quite simply beyond me. Now some months (and many nights of broken sleep) on, Hill's unwieldy tome still seems unreviewable. The testimony of other reviewers confirms it. 'How does one do justice to a collection that is not so much a book as a cosmos?' Daniel Johnson asked in *Standpoint Magazine*. Bringing together twenty-one books of poetry (including four new works: *Ludo, Expostulations On The Volcano, Liber Illustrium Virorum*, and *Al Tempo De' Tremuoti*) and with three sequences 'greatly revised and expanded', it will take years for readers to labour through it. 'Much of his later work would benefit from a council of scholars, or just a dedicated wiki',

William Logan wrote in his review: 'the late poems are so often unforgiving, few readers will pass muster'. When Hill, in his most recent lecture as Oxford Professor of Poetry, quotes Isaac Rosenberg on the nature of poetry we might very well hear the chime of our own predicament as readers of Hill's vast, tortuously re-conceived *oeuvre*: 'I know it is beyond my reach just now, except, perhaps, in bits.'

'Like trying to summarise a Beethoven quartet', is how Donald Hall, reviewing Hill's *Tenebrae* in 1980, defined the impossibility of trying to paraphrase a Hill poem. Decades on, performing a reading of Shakespeare's Sonnet 66, Hill would ask his Oxford audience: 'How'd you paraphrase that? You don't.' For the total effect 'cannot be paraphrased. It can only be delivered by the words and the metrical pulses'. Rather than commit the same heresy of paraphrase in what follows here, I shall instead follow the poet-as-professor's lead and listen in to a poem that has been working on me with (to quote Longley) 'increasing pleasure' and may therefore be instrumental in a short review such as this. From the profoundly elegiac *Al Tempo De' Tremuoti*, 'Sei Madrigali' comes as a quietly seismic late-career performance. First published in 2010 in *Standpoint* magazine, it appears slightly revised here (Hill, like Yeats, a re-maker of self and song), dedicated to the 'PMH' who will be familiar to readers since 2006's *Without Title*. Pointing up Hill's obsession with musical forms and procedures – the madrigal being a song for several voices that makes use of elaborate counterpoint – each 'madrigal' is composed of two sinuous quatrains rhyming *abba*, with the first opening on a question:

> Is it not strange that thou shouldst weep? So gravid
> The sweetest song a burdening: the six
> *Metamorphoses*, of violence and sex,
> The sensuous oboe touched by sensual Ovid.

Readers will recognise the question as that asked of Apollo by Mnemosyne, the muse of memory, in Keats's unfinished epic *Hyperion: A Fragment*. Here, however, there is a twist, as Mnemosyne's 'So gifted', becomes in Hill's playfully complicating hands, 'So gravid', as the motifs of sex, death and creative death-in-life dovetail from the start; the poet feeling intently the weight of the world and of words. Hill's most recent Oxford lecture had him quote Keats on the workings of repetition and memory and that other meaning of 'burden' is invoked here in a work that ingeniously re-orchestrates remembered melodies and motifs: the music of memory and of ideas is one of constant modulation and metamorphosis. With the entrance in the third line of Benjamin Britten's 1951 work for solo oboe *Six Metamorphoses after Ovid*, that 'sensuous oboe' not only rehearses Hill's Miltonic sense of poetry itself as 'Simple, sensuous and passionate' but also reminds us of his 'envy' of the composer who, as he once remarked in interview, 'unites solitary meditation with direct, sensuous communication to a greater degree than the poet'. In shaping these as 'madrigals' Hill is thereby straining after the same 'sensuous configurations of sound' even as he remains keenly aware of his own artistic limitations. Crucially 'false-relationed' (note, for instance, the punning clash of 'lyre' and 'lure' in this stanza), 'Sei Madrigali' confirms Hill as a staggeringly gifted student of dissonance in the manner of John Dowland, whose lute song 'Lasso vita mia' lights up the fourth madrigal.

'Up against ageing and dying I stand bemused / by labours of flight: a low-geared heron / retiring to its pool', Hill wrote in *The Orchards of Syon* (2002) and the second madrigal repeats this ascending motif as the observant poet notes: 'The heron's flight out of the reeds is laggard / Yet still it climbs.' Testifying to Hill's poetics of reciprocity, that word 'laggard' calls out to another of his presiding spirits, GM Hopkins, whose sonnet 'To R.B.' was the subject of the Oxford lecture of March 2014. Importantly for Hill it is a sonnet 'about creative laggardness' in which we see Hopkins 'presenting the act of begetting and conceiving a poem in language that summons to itself thoughts of sexuality and procreation'. Here, again, this madrigal with its repeated 'too late' and repetition of the key note 'grief' – '... and I / Display too late my early grief' – articulates Hill's overriding concern with both artistic and sexual failure: the relationship never consummated, the work aborted, the consummate artist anguished by questions having to do with art's purpose, his own creative impotence, and the disappointments of the age and of old age. It matters to Hill that so many of Hopkins's poems are 'fragments', as he observes how it is, oxymoronically, the artist's inability to write that engenders the poem itself and the one immortal line that proves all of the poet's labours of song worthwhile: 'What I find so moving in the poem is the near-defiance of sterility carried in the sensuous, intrinsic beauty of that glowing line: "Leaves yet the mind a mother of immortal song".'

The air is full of sonorous energy as Giulio Caccini's *madrigale* 'Amarilli, mia bella' resonates through the fourth madrigal in a redolent moment of bell-clear autobiographical recall. Tellingly, this is one of the moments that was reworked by Hill for book publication – the once 'warped seventy-eight / Bucking the needle' becoming the 'scuffed seventy-eight'. That that 'scuffed' summons back the half-lit half-life of childhood – 'At nightfall // My father scuffed clay into the house' – in 'The Stone Man' from *King Log* (1968) seems appropriate: Hill's living body of work is above all a passionate labour of love concerned from the beginning with sounding the roots and origins of our selves, our language and the structures we live by. Pulled back into the past, the fifth madrigal ends:

> If we should labour back against time's motion
> Still distant are those lovers we were not.

It is the lines that do the work, or 'labour', of keeping the would-be lovers so heartbreakingly apart. The insinuating line-break (a trademark Hill manoeuvre) engineers that fatal, breathtaking moment of hesitation ('motion / Still') as the pivot-word 'still' with its two opposing meanings holds the lovers ambiguously suspended in time, for all time, denying resolution. Moreover, the syntax itself thwarts the flow of sense just as the lovers themselves have been, and continue to be, thwarted: 'Still distant are those lovers we were not' is more tortured than, say, 'those lovers we were not are still distant'. As Hill professed recently at Oxford: 'it is the aim and function of poetry so to move us, perhaps to move us to a rapt stillness', the poem's syntax being 'of major significance' in effecting this feat of technique.

'*I can see someone walking there, a girl,* / And she is you, old love', the poem's final stanza opens reprising Sosostris's words from Michael Tippett's 1955 quest opera *The Midsummer Marriage*. Hijacked from TS Eliot's *The Waste Land*, the clairvoyant Sosostris stands for artistic inspiration itself as she guides the protagonists on a journey towards enlightenment and self-understanding. It is one of Hill's persistent themes too; the artist-as-lover striving for truth and self-knowledge. Elusive and allusive, 'Sei Madrigali' is both haunted and vivified by art and its circuitous, unanswerable questions – Yeats, Britten, Coventry Patmore, Hopkins, Keats, Eliot, Dowland, Caccini, Tippett are among Hill's summoned sources of animation – but it is to the memory of Hill's own *oeuvre* that this richly resourced meditation on the creative process is finally most indebted. As the poem closes –

> ... Edging the meadow
> The may-tree is all light and all shadow.
> Coming and going are the things eternal.

– we are thrown back to lines from *The Orchards of Syon*, the collection described by Hill as being 'about depth of memory and broken memory':

> How beautiful the world unrecognized
> through most of seventy years, the may-tree filling
> with visionary silent laughter.
>
> – *Orchards*, V

Thus it ends with the poet in old age ghosted by that long-ago broken-off love in a way that might seem reminiscent of Fanny Brawne's eternal hold on Keats: 'I eternally see her figure eternally vanishing'. It reminds us, finally, of Hill as love poet, perhaps the 'Latin love / elegist' of *The Orchard's* 'tenebrous thresholds' (LIV) who resides out on the 'verge' (that being the final word in *Broken Hierarchies* as the sequence breaks off without a full-stop) between worlds composing lines of force that turn and return with infinite variation.

What then may be Hill's motive in giving the world this staggering record of artistic creation and failure with its many revisions to the life and work, its rewrites, retakes, rememberings and dismemberings? To show us, perhaps, that art is living, in process, never final, that it partakes of the 'things eternal' and that the labours it demands both test and delight us as thinking, sensual beings. 'The writing and criticism in depth of poetry is an essential, even a vital practice', Hill recently proclaimed: 'We are in our public life desperately in need of the energy of intelligence created by these pursuits.' That the work of this astonishing, tremendous poet will be read generations from now is certain. It is the work of a lifetime. For now, we must make do with our imperfect knowledge and summon our own energy of intelligence in the face of its remorseless, exhilarating music. This is art that pushes us to the brink of our own capacities: 'understandable and still ungraspable'.

James Aitchison

CARSELAND DIARY

Every morning for a week – ten days? I should keep a diary. A
scrim of white-frilled ice covered the pond.

I should keep a diary of snowdrops, crocuses, aconites, daffodils,
hazel catkins and hellebores. I chant the names when no one is
listening.

I celebrate the little festival of light around the middle of February
when the Carse tilts to catch the steeper angle of the sun.

In March the water level in the pond was as high as the stepping
stones. March was a hot dry month on the Carse last year.

The pear was the first fruit tree to flower this year. I should keep a
diary. Ground-frost is air-frost on the lower levels of the Carse.
White petals blackened overnight.

I felt no warmth in the April sun. I raised my right hand in reflex
salute to shade my eyes from the glare and dry my tears. The sky
was blue and imperturbable.

I should note the date of the first honey-bee – a single bee or one
bee at a time? – to nuzzle the pieris flowers' white cluster-bells.
Perhaps bees waggle-dance only when catmint blossom-time begins.

The soil in May was too cold for seeds to germinate and yet fruit-
buds were swelling on apple trees, plum trees, gooseberry bushes
and raspberry canes; half-promise of a daze of harvesting. I chant
the names when no one is listening.

I should keep records of the weights of fruits and the plucking days
from July to November. But not in leaner years when measuring
would be discourteous.

I should note the date of the first incoming skein of grey lag geese,
and the final mowing of the half-moon lawn.

Lucy Ingrams

TODAY ...

... you watch the sea from the window, while I study grasses –
moths led me to them: I'd gone out looking for bright breaths
of flower and come back tuned to fine-jointed staves,
shy-coloured panicles. My grass book, which thrives
on the dry, tells me (in millimetres) of common
couch culms, when you tell me we've lost the horizon.
We stare, mourning dimension – flat as the waves'
skin / the sky's hang now a low fleece
of fog wraps the chord-line between them
                                            until
I try this: tail you to the fields, lie us down, show you the frail
fastenings, like hair, weaving Earth to the air, turn
us over, find out small hollows among the stems – a lichen
scrape, a whisking feather, a skylark's gaze, hummocks of heather –
and slowly, our seeing cups again, regains curvature.

Lucy Ingrams

Like throwing sixes – the double
    luck of summer
and a Sunday brings me
    to the water meadows early.

Behind the willows, the river
    stutters into miked-up rhythms
from a cox's whip of words: *Keep
    the power on, the power on!*

Late, rather – was it spring I last
    came here? With you? – the ash
has fruited its keys already, the grass
    stoops hay-high, wired with crickets.

Careful, I touch my thought
    across one wound-site that you
left behind. Nothing. Nearly. Can
    you-in-me really heal?

Water mint, yarrow, knapweed –
    back through staunchnesses
of mind, seep names forgotten
    with last autumn.

*Think about those hands being level,
    so the boat stays level!*
        I put mine out,
            steady myself,

            I'm not used to walking without
        the stiffness of our pain.

Across the bridge, the brambles
    are in flower.

# Dairena Ní Chinnéide

BAINEANN
   – do Lá Idirnáisiúnta na mBan

Baineann baineannacht
le bláthú
le scéalta súgacha
meanma do mheoin
suan do linbh
daonnacht draíochtúil do dheirfiúr
anam aoibhinn d'aintín
cluais chabharthach do chara.

Baineann baineannacht
le grá
le haontas na haithne
is cneasú ar arraing
mórtas na máthar
spleodar na hanama
torthúlacht na talún
éirim na héisteachta.

Baineann baineannacht
le cré is croí lán
le croíthe briste
is oícheanta lán ghealaí
géire intinne
bua na híobartha
uaisle tuisceana
saoirse na spleodarachta.

Baineann baineannacht
led inscne
d'insint féin
ar shaol do bheatha
deirge do chuid fola
athrú in aois do cholainne
taibhrimhí timthriallacha d'aigne
síor athrú agus fás fada fairsing.

## 'EACH POEM IS A WORLD ENTIRE': EILÉAN NÍ CHUILLEANÁIN INTERVIEWED BY SIEN DELTOUR

Eiléan Ní Chuilleanáin's collections with The Gallery Press include *Acts and Monuments* (1972), *The Rose Geranium* (1981), *The Magdalene Sermon* (1989), *The Brazen Serpent* (1994), *Selected Poems* (2008) and *The Sun-Fish* (2009). Her most recent collection is *The Boys of Bluehill* (2015). She has won the Patrick Kavanagh Award, *The Irish Times* Award for Poetry, the O'Shaughnessy Award of the Irish-American Cultural Institute, and the 2010 International Griffin Poetry Prize, for *The Sun-Fish*. She is a Fellow and Professor of English (Emeritus) at Trinity College, Dublin, a member of Aosdána, and a founding-editor of the literary journal *Cyphers*.

**Sien Deltour**: My first question is about religion, because rituals and convents are quite common in your poetry. In the poem 'Vertigo' in *The Sun-Fish* (2009), there is a shift between generations, from a generation that still has faith to a generation that thinks that all these rituals and pilgrimages are a little old-fashioned. How is faith changing?

**Eiléan Ní Chuilleanáin**: I don't think that 'Vertigo' has anything to do with faith. I think that poem is about a generational difference; it is about a woman who has a certain kind of religion which is focused on things like pilgrimages and rosary beads. I don't go into the question of what the daughters believe, because what they're mostly thinking is what a nuisance their mother is. So, I don't think it's about faith. Nobody mentions spiritual experience until the end where the woman has a vision of quite a different sort.

**SD**: Which is interesting, because she indeed has a vision, but you never really know what it is.

**ENC**: Yes, I think it's death. That is what she sees.

**SD**: In the poem 'The Witch in the Wardrobe', there is a reference to CS Lewis's Narnia. What does Narnia mean to you, and what do you think about Lewis's views on Christianity and the way he portrays it in his books?

**ENC**: Because I am so interested in the literature of the Renaissance, what interests me is that, like a Renaissance writer, Lewis combines Christianity, in which he does believe, with myth, in which he doesn't. I think he was trying to write about death, which is a very difficult thing to do in a book for children, although, of course, it is done. I really like his *The Lion, the Witch and the Wardrobe*, *The Magician's Nephew* and *The Horse and his Boy*. That last one is, I think, about the difference between Northern and Southern Ireland. These are books I read as a child and children's books are terribly important to me.

SD: Because of your mother's profession?[1]

ENC: Partly because of my mother's profession. Partly, I suppose, because I started thinking about ideas for poetry when I was very young, and found those in myth, folklore, children's books.

SD: You also use a lot of myths and legends, a lot of Irish legends, in *The Sun-Fish* (2009). These myths could be considered in the context of spirituality, which is a very hazy term. Could we say that these types of stories are spiritual, as people use them to make sense of life and death?

ENC: I suppose you could, yes. I think in a way that that book is less hung up on myth than some of the earlier poems. In 'The Sun-Fish', I was trying to write about scientific material and about history. But yes, I am sure that myth is not so much a way of trying to express as trying to define what one cannot express, or trying to define what one cannot understand, or what one cannot make sense of.

SD: Your poetry tends to be evasive; you write about something without mentioning it or by circling around it. I thought I could relate that to your poems about people who have died, but who are still present in a way.

ENC: Simply because of my age, there are people who have died that I feel I am still in touch with, but I don't feel that I've really successfully begun to write about them. Although, I suppose I did in the one poem about my father, in which I have got that one incident from his youth.

SD: That's 'On Lacking the Killer Instinct' in *The Sun-Fish*?

ENC: Yes, that's right. I suppose I am trying not to say more than I can about my subjects. So, as in many cases, what my poem is saying is: *Look, this is there; for example, death. This is how we feel around it, but we do not know what it is.*

SD: It's something you repeat in poems like 'The Water', I think, when you say 'this is real'[2], this moment is real. Is that what you mean?

ENC: Yes. Because people talk about something being only a trick of the light as if that means it isn't real, but the trick, the light, is real, the light by which we see things.

SD: That makes me think about impressionist art. For example, Monet, who painted one image at different times in the day, as the light changed. I thought I saw that in your poetry as well.

ENC: Yes. I suppose when I was reading art history as a teenager, the pictures that I saw, in quite a limited experience at that stage, would have included things like the Lane pictures[3] which are now in the Municipal Gallery, but which were then in the Tate, because the Tate Gallery in London wouldn't give them up. And works like Renoir's *Les Parapluies*, or the one that a friend of my husband's actually stole out of the Tate[4], Berthe Morisot's *Jour d'Été*, just two women in a boat and sparkling water behind and all around them. They were what I knew of art at that stage, and that has stayed with me.

SD: I can certainly see that influence in poems like 'The Water' and 'Where the Pale Flower Flashes and Disappears' in *The Sun-Fish*. There are also some recurrent words in that collection, such as 'arched'. You talk about the 'arched ways'[5] of writing, trying to see past what is there. You describe, for example, the door in the poem 'The Door' as a 'celestial arch'[6] because it reveals more at one point.

ENC: I think I dream about arches. The best and most interesting pieces of architecture, certainly, were in churches where I grew up. If they were not very good themselves they were gestures towards something that was wonderful. Churches that were built in the nineteenth century after Catholic emancipation in Ireland would all be gestures to the Gothic style or the Baroque style, and they were often much more elaborate and interesting, certainly, than the vernacular, household architecture of the other buildings around me.

SD: In 'Daniel Grose' (*The Brazen Serpent*, 1994), a painter is making a drawing and at the same time looking for the human figure. Is the human figure that which makes the space live, and makes it interesting?

ENC: Oh, I think so. It's all about scale. I think in any picture, and in any imagined picture also, it is important to have some kind of human figure, whether far or near.

SD: A lot of your poems are set in Ireland or Italy. Do you always have a place in the back of your mind when you write a poem?

ENC: A sense of place is something that helps the reader, isn't it? I wouldn't say that I absolutely always have a sense of place in poems, but I'm sure that where I do, it helps.

SD: It reminds me of the 'mimetic space' of a poem,[7] the kind of anchorage to reality a poem always has. There is a space in which your poem, and its meaning, can evolve.

ENC: You go into a space and something has to have changed by the time you come out of it. I think that is sort of a description of a poem.

SD: In *The Sun-Fish* there are a lot of doors, windows, water surfaces and even mirrors. Still, I never get a sense of so-called 'in-betweenness', a popular term in postcolonial literature. No one is ever really stuck between two places, between England and Ireland, for example.

ENC: I don't think I can claim that. There are plenty of Irish writers who can, but not someone with the kind of background that I had. I do have a quite strong self-identification with the nation rather than being perched somewhere outside of it.

SD: Languages also seem to be important in your poetry. You even mention languages of nature, such as the language of birds.

ENC: Well, that is a folktale theme, isn't it, being able to understand the language of birds. It's in the Siegfried myth, but also in Irish. To me, learning languages is something you can go on and on and on with, because you can always learn them better and you can always learn more languages and you will never come to the end of it.

SD: Knowing both English and Irish, do you feel that you are a stranger to both languages in some way?

ENC: I would hardly say that and yet ... I often think I am rather bold in saying that I feel I know Italian, although it is a language I speak quite a lot. But, at the same time, there are huge areas of the language and the culture that I don't know about, but I feel that, certainly in both English and Irish, I know as much as most people. I do think that, for me, Irish and English means a choice, constantly choosing a word. Will I say this in English or will I say this in Irish?

SD: There is one poem in *The Sun-Fish*, 'In His Language', of which the second part seems to be about the language your son uses. It's about music and there is a beat in the poem, the ringing 'in the floorboards'[8].

ENC: My sister, who died, was a musician at a very high level. We always used to say that she played the violin because my mother played the cello during her pregnancy. When I was growing up, you would always hear somebody practising in the house and it was lovely, and, nowadays, I hear my son practising.

SD: In some poems you also use language to take on a voice that is not yours. You try, for example, to talk for the Magdalenes, but I don't think you impose yourself.

ENC: No, I don't want to talk for them, because I have no right. But I want to hear them, I want to imagine what their voice might have been. There are certain kinds of poetry that really annoy me. When somebody imagines what it must be like to be a Greek fisherman or something like that. People should be aware of how impossible it is to imagine and yet, in some ways, how necessary. I think too much poetry is written without any sense of that gap, of the strain that it is to imagine another person's life.

SD: Some of your poems are about historical events. Do you try to link those up with personal experience? For example in 'Ballinascarthy' and, I think, also in 'The Sun-Fish', there always seems to be a personal aspect.

ENC: People talk about my mother's family all the time, probably because of their connection with the revolution, but my father's family was interesting too, though nobody recorded very much about that. So, in a way, a lot of that poem is just quite literal. I came upon this place associated with his people, and I was quite astonished to find this little bit of poetry written up in Irish about a battle there I'd never heard of.[9]

SD: There is a line in 'Ballinascarthy' about the trees whistling a tune through which you hear the voices of the deceased in the battle. In fact, trees are mentioned in several poems, especially in 'The Water'.

ENC: Certainly trees are a wonderful image because they have their underground and their overground. The character of trees varies so much from one country to another, depending on things like the wind and the kind of trees the people plant and the need for shade. And trees in convents and colleges are different from trees outside convents and colleges.

SD: This idea of linking worlds is also visible in 'A Bridge Between Two Counties' (*The Sun-Fish*), which is, I think, a poem very much about death and how to deal with it. And I again discovered your interest in ritual, because the people who cross the bridge encounter barrels and planks which slow their voyage. Is this a way to stall the confrontation with death?

ENC: In some ways, yes. I think death certainly comes into it. A memory is a very important part of it. When my parents first met in 1939, they were both working in an Irish college in Co Waterford where there is a very small Gaeltacht area. The nearest town is in Co Cork, so there is a bridge between two counties. The bus used to stop on one side and people would have to walk across and get into another bus on the other side. And I remember the cars going slowly across between these barriers because they were afraid the bridge would fall down, and it is the mercy of God it didn't. So, the slowing down may be part of it, but it was also based on a story about an adoption in London. Some friends when they lived in London had been asked to take in an Irish girl who was pregnant. They took her in and she went off and had her baby in hospital. Then she came back with the baby (and this was all being arranged through a Catholic charity), and one day the husband went out with the baby and he was told to go to Waterloo Bridge and walk across the bridge and there would be somebody waiting on the other side. He just handed the baby over and that was the end of it as far as they were concerned.

SD: So that is also part of the image of disappearing in the mist, and the mother who keeps the baby alive in her memory?

ENC: In her mind, yes. That's one side of it, but then somebody who read the poem said that she thought it was about my mother sort of helping my sister, across into her own death. And I thought, well that's not what I thought it was about, but maybe it is all the same, certainly because I brought in my sister's funeral, and Val Kennedy, a man of eighty, saying: 'She will live / Forever in my memory'[10]. It was strange to me. I thought: 'She is dead at forty-six; how long do you think you are going to live?'

SD: Is memory a part of language that is performative? By remembering someone, do you keep them alive? Is it a bit of a paradox that you try to keep someone alive and remember them, while all the time actually changing them?

ENC: I can see logically why that might be so. I notice, for example, that a lot of people still talk to me about my mother, because she was a very forceful personality. She would give people advice and they would take it, which none of her children ever did. My father is somebody much more private; I don't talk about him as often. Perhaps that's the difference, I remember him, but apart from my brother – who is much younger than me and therefore had a different experience – I don't have the same opportunity to revise his character, so to speak.

SD: Other people will give their own view on your poetry as well. Does that change your perspective on your work?

ENC: Yes. I've found myself more than once beginning to read some critical remark and thinking they got it quite wrong and then, by the end of it, thinking: *Actually, all that is there in the poem.* I hadn't seen it, but it is there.

SD: In a way it's again about perspective, about how you look at things. In your poem 'Fireman's Lift' there is a line where you step back to look at something. You say 'We saw the work entire'[11], you see it from a different angle. Is it necessary to look at a poet's work in its entirety to understand the parts or do you think that when you read one poem, you already have a sense of what this poet is about?

ENC: Oh I think so. I think each poem is a world entire. I wrote 'Fireman's Lift' when my mother was dying and I realised when it happened that first of all it was entirely appropriate for me to write about her, because as a writer herself she didn't mind being written about. And then also that, when I was young, I tried to write about great big subjects, especially about great big paintings. There is a 'Last Judgment' in Munich, a Rubens, and I remember trying to write about it when I was about twenty-two and making a miserable failure of it. And when I started to write that poem 'Fireman's Lift', I suddenly realised I now have the poetic confidence and the poetic instrument that enables me to write about a picture in a way that I couldn't when I was younger.

SD: In a poem like 'The Witch in the Wardrobe', in which you very clearly say that a door is being opened, you are actually, I think, writing about another world you step into as a reader. Is that what a poem should be about, giving a glimpse or a view of something else, something other?

ENC: I think not just the poem, but a lot of literature is about another world, another perspective, something that arouses an appetite in the reader. It is a very sensual poem and I wanted to suggest that it is like a bodily appetite. If one can imagine oneself reading certain novels for the first time, that kind of excitement, it's like a hunger.

SD: Because in this poem the reader is kind of invaded by that other world?

ENC: Yes, that's it.

SD: The other worlds of the past and the future: do your poems imagine those worlds as a way of dealing with them?

ENC: I think the past is what we know. We hardly know the present and we can project the future, but it is a blueprint, it is without colour. The past is full of textures. I look out of that window [*in the Irish College in Leuven*] and I almost expect my aunt [*who was a nun in Belgium*] to be walking up and down, reading her prayer book, because that is something real that I carry with me. The future is so unimaginable for all of us. Even if you plan carefully and you follow your plan and it all works out, you couldn't know what it would be like when it happened. And life is full of these decisions, like the decision to have a child or in my case to adopt a child, you know. 'What on earth was I thinking of?' I say to myself.

SD: I hope you know that by now.

ENC: Well, I don't know what I was thinking of. I know what has happened and that is what's important.

SD: The surface again seems to be more important than what is beyond that. In 'The Sun-Fish', for example, the surface of the water is mentioned. The sun-fish are always pressing against this screen or 'screed' of water, and one cannot look beyond it, because what is simply there is truly important.

ENC: Yes, I mean, the sun-fish is a basking shark. All we know about it is what is on the surface. People don't really know, for example, how they reproduce and why they can disappear for years and then just suddenly reappear in large numbers. There is a big 'how is it?' that we do not know.

SD: There is a sense of cyclicality, I think, in that poem – the sun-fish disappearing and coming back again – which is also part of life.

ENC: And it is also part of history. Those people in the poem fishing for the sun-fish were so poor, it was such a scruffy, miserable industry and they were desperate. When the sun-fish came back everything had changed, life had changed and people were living better.

SD: Is this idea of cyclicality something you use a lot in your poetry?

ENC: I would try not to place too much emphasis on it, because I think what we experience is linear. It was like this and then it was like this and then it was like something else. And yes, there are moments when you rediscover things from the past, but I wouldn't like to make that a part of my programme.

SD: You're recognised as one of the first female poets in contemporary Ireland. Some critics say you had to assert yourself not only as a poet but also as a woman poet, and that you helped clear the way for the next generation.

ENC: I think there is some truth in that. Of course there is one very important predecessor who writes in Irish, Máire Mhac an tSaoi, a splendid poet, whose 1956 collection, *Margadh na Saoire*, included a very striking translation of a poem by Lorca. So that would have influenced me, the knowledge that there was somebody there doing it. I am a bit older, but Eavan Boland had a book out before me. In my early years as a poet people used to say that I was not really a woman at all, that I was a kind of a male impersonator, because I was not writing about gynaecology and I was not writing about domestic matters. I was writing perhaps more adventurous poems. Or perhaps I was writing more out of my imagination.

SD: But at the same time, there is a kind of femininity in your poetry.

ENC: Oh yes. In my first book there is not that much that expresses femininity as such. It took a while for me to find not so much a female voice, because it was always my voice and I was always female, but to insist that it was female, to draw the right kind of attention to the female voice.

SD: In *The Sun-Fish*, femininity or the feminine voice is not really explicit, but there is the aspect of the sea and water. Is that a feminine element in your poetry? Because you once said that things that contain other things are feminine, like relics and the hollow tower you write about.[12]

ENC: Yes, that was explicitly meant to be a feminist image. The sea, I suppose, is such a vast idea that you can make it signify many things like time, the world, death, maybe also the feminine. A lot of those poems about the sea reflect my relationship with my first boyfriend, a marine biologist. He was the first person I ever heard talking about ecology when nobody knew much about it. I was obsessed with this man who was obsessed with the sea. I was reading Conrad because Conrad was his favourite writer, and I was taking in all these ideas about the sea. And I think also maybe because of the position of Ireland, as an island. We have this great big, long coastline which is quite different, say, from some continental countries that may have a little bit of coastline here or there.

SD: The sea is a part of nature and nature seems to always play a role in your poetry. Is the most interesting thing about nature the collision with humans, with culture?

ENC: Oh yes, that's what we know about. We don't know about nature when it's on its own. It's when the fisherman, or the artist, or the pilgrim confronts nature that language emerges; we have to say something about it.

SD: An image you use a lot is that of the spider, which you explicitly refer to in the poem 'Agnes Bernelle 1923-1999'. You write that it is the creature you like the most, because it makes its 'own new centre every day'.[13] Can that be linked up with how you write poetry and how your poems always have a different centre?

ENC: I think so. I think it is a good image for the poet, because with each poem you are trying to make something complete and for a moment you think you've done it, and then the next day it doesn't look quite so complete so you start again. I wish I could do one every day, but obviously it takes much longer. Also, it is perfectly true, I love spiders!

SD: At what point do you think of a title for a poem?

ENC: It would depend, very much. For something like 'The Sun-Fish' or 'The Polio Epidemic', I thought: *I want to write a poem about this*. Obviously the original, more usual, name for the sun-fish is the basking shark, but 'The Sun-Fish' seemed like a good idea. It is a nicer word and then it also made a title for the collection. I think I probably do think of titles, now you ask me, at a very early stage, because that also gives an extra impetus to the poem.

SD: The structure of the whole volume, is that something you think about consciously?

ENC: No, I would try not to think about it too much as I write the individual poems, and then usually there is a stage where I get them all out and read them all, and I think well this goes with this, and then usually at that stage I get further ideas for other poems and I would write those, as it were, to fill gaps. Not quite to fill gaps, but they are called into being by the poems in the collection.

SD: The reader has to invest quite a lot in your poetry, because you can read it and not understand a thing at first sight. Do you keep your audience in mind while writing?

Still from *The Floating World*: 'Dust 1' (2013)

**Clare Langan**'s *The Floating World* (infra-red video, duration 15 minutes) is a three-screen digital installation presenting a poetic message about possible futures and our place in the world. Shot in three contrasting locations, the viewer is led through haunting and elegiac landscapes where white ash, snow and dust swirl and settle, prompting thoughts of a world devastated and beyond habitation. *The Floating World* questions the relationship between mankind and the planet. The installation had its Irish premiere at VISUAL Carlow in January 2015. Images are available as limited edition prints.

W. www.clarelangan.com    E. info@clarelangan.com

Still from *The Floating World:* 'Dubai Triptych 1', (2013), left panel

Still from *The Floating World*: 'Dubai Triptych 1' (2013), centre panel

Still from *The Floating World:* 'Skelligs Triptych 1' (2013), left panel

Still from *The Floating World:* 'Skelligs Triptych 1' (2013), centre panel

Still from *The Floating World:* 'Dust 2 – Buried House' (2013)

Still from *The Floating World:* 'Dust 3' (2013)

Still from *The Floating World:* 'Lost City 1' (2013)

**Clare Langan** studied Fine Art at the National College of Art and Design, Dublin, and, with a Fulbright Scholarship, completed a film workshop at NYU. She has represented Ireland in numerous international Biennales. Her film *Metamorphosis* (2007) won the Principal Prize at Oberhausen International Short Film Festival, Germany, while *The Floating World* was awarded the Prix Videoformes 2014 at VIDEOFORMES 2014, Clermont-Ferrand, France. Her films and photographs are in a number of international public and private collections, including The Irish Museum of Modern Art, The Arts Council of Ireland, The Office of Public Works, the Tony Podesta Private Collection, Washington, and the Hugo and Carla Brown Collection in the UK. She is currently completing a permanent large-scale photographic and video installation commissioned for NUI, Maynooth. See **www.clarelangan.com**

ENC: I think I do. When I first wrote poetry I wasn't thinking of the reader and it was terribly obscure. And then I began to be published and I began to think: 'Oh well, I'd better make this a bit clearer.' So, I tried to go on and do that, but then critics still said that my poetry was terribly obscure. And then along comes Medbh McGuckian and all of a sudden my poetry became much clearer, because hers seemed really obscure and that has kind of remained. I find now that readers are prepared to take a bit more trouble than they were in the 1970s.

SD: Do you think it's a shame that poetry is so little read by the mainstream audience?

ENC: In Ireland that's not so much the case. Though I'm afraid that I've just recently noticed that students seem to be less interested in poetry than they were. But I think in fact poetry gets a lot of academic attention and people still come to poetry readings. They seem to be interested.

SD: But still, a lot more people read novels than poetry?

ENC: I suppose so. I think in Ireland people may read more poetry than elsewhere. The provost of Trinity says his brothers, who are farmers in Co Wexford, sit around the pub throwing poems at each other in the evenings. So, there may be a bit more popular interest. Now, these wouldn't be poems like mine, but they might be poems by Yeats or Kavanagh, that they learned at school. One of the bestsellers recently in the Irish bookshops was called *Favourite Poems We Learned in School*, a reprint of the poems that were taught in schools maybe thirty years ago, and I think that is quite interesting, that people went out and bought that book because they wanted to read those poems again.

SD: Maybe out of some kind of nostalgia?

ENC: Yes, but also because they really liked them. I think with poetry, people expect to return to it, whereas they're less likely to read a novel twice.

SD: Is that why you write poetry and not, for example, fiction?

ENC: Fiction is hard work, you have to sit down every day and write. I began to write poetry because I wanted to do better than my mother. At that age, you know, you are twelve or thirteen, you think: 'Well she can do that, I'll do something harder.' I write poetry because I love reading poetry and I want to produce that experience.

SD: A final question then, about something I heard a while ago. *A poet writes to become someone he was not before the act of writing, and when the poem is written the poet is someone else, and does not remember the one he was before.* Is that something you can relate to?

ENC: I'd have to think about that. Now that I'm seventy, I think I would have had to become so many different people over the years. Certainly I feel that as a poet I am a somewhat different person from who I am, for example, as a retired academic. But I think I'd have to consider whether what you say is true.

### Notes

1 Eilís Dillon, novelist and children's author.
2 Eiléan Ní Chuilleanáin, *The Sun-Fish* (The Gallery Press, 2009), p. 38.
3 Hugh Lane was an important collector of impressionist paintings and is best-known for establishing Dublin's Municipal Gallery of Modern Art in 1908. (www.hughlane.ie/hugh-lane-1875-1915)
4 On 12 April 1956 Paul Hogan and Bill Fogarty stole *Jour d'Été* from the Tate Gallery to draw attention to the claim of the Municipal Gallery in Dublin to the Lane pictures, which Lane had left to the gallery in an (unwitnessed) codicil. (http://comeheretome.com/2012/11/09/hugh-lane-painting-robbery-1956/)
5 Eiléan Ní Chuilleanáin, *The Sun-Fish* (The Gallery Press, 2009), p. 36.
6 Eiléan Ní Chuilleanáin, *The Sun-Fish* (The Gallery Press, 2009), p. 18.
7 See David Gullentops, *Poétique du lisuel* (Paris-Méditerranée, 2001), pp. 140-143.
8 Eiléan Ní Chuilleanáin, *The Sun-Fish* (The Gallery Press, 2009), p. 29.
9 The inscription by Pádraig Óg Ó Scolaidhe starts off the poem 'Ballinascarthy': *Is marach an dream úd Caithness dob' ag Gaeil a bhí an lá.* The 'Battle of the Big Cross' was fought in Clonakilty, during the rebellion of 1798.
10 Eiléan Ní Chuilleanáin, *The Sun-Fish* (The Gallery Press, 2009), p. 13.
11 Eiléan Ní Chuilleanáin, *The Brazen Serpent* (The Gallery Press, 1994), p. 10.
12 The poem is called 'The Lady's Tower' and is part of the volume *Site of Ambush* (1975).
13 Eiléan Ní Chuilleanáin, *The Girl Who Married the Reindeer* (The Gallery Press, 2001), p. 43.

This interview took place at the Irish College, Leuven, Belgium, on 01/03/2013

Jennifer A McGowan

THE SCALE OF THINGS

The snake is green, and knows it.
Uncoiling, she solves the knot of her body
and proceeds, leisurely, through sunlit dapples,
viridian grass, the woods' rustling hush.

Bending, one might catch the shade
of her S where it kisses the ground.
But of her takings, her hungers – nothing.
What it must be to be so unmarked.

And when, expansive, she leaves behind
the palest shadow of herself, it is only that
which, haunted, we keep, and not her
coiled question, her hidden tangle.

Dan O'Brien

THE WAR REPORTER PAUL WATSON ON THE IDEA OF THE ABSURD

*It's July again so I've got corpses*
*on my mind.* A friend's tasked with shepherding
Dan Eldon's young body home. Other friends
stoned and stabbed. The liaison officer
says rules is rules and we can only move
bodies in regulation body bags.
Our friend fumes. The fan ticks. Everybody
knows how it feels to go to a funeral
for a friend, laid out there like she's not there
and yet she is, she fucking *was.* But how
can it feel to barter for hostages
in the blister of Bakara Market
when the ransom that they want is so small
that you know you've come too late? The perfume
in his Cobra T-shirt. Pure in the bed
of our galloping truck, the whip-smart cracks
of bullets, the boy singing, *Whenever*
*I feel afraid, I hold my head erect*
*and whistle.* Their bodies were recovered
from a trash heap in July. Now twenty
years ago today. That soldier remained
unswayed. Regulations. A man with heart
would've offered to clean them up before
their families would be collecting them from
the shimmering tarmac in Nairobi,
before Dan Eldon's burnt body would ash
ribbons through the limbs of acacias
rising up like ancestors from the tail-
end of Ngong Hills. Our friend asked how much
for some regulation body bags, then?
The officer enjoyed this. We don't sell
our body bags. Ha ha ha. *Remind me*
*to include this in our pitch, Dan, so that*
*executives in Hollywood will know*
*what I mean by the absurd.*

Tadhg Russell

Harbour lights glittered as our ferry docked,
and stars too, then headlights. When the cars crept
away in every direction, a full moon hung low,
peering over rooftops, a whole continent sleeping,
and each of us travelling inland, past cities and towns,
habitation thinning out, all contact down to one voice
on the radio, and would anyone recognise the spot
they were destined, except for a familiar quiet
that gathers at the centre of every life; if you listen
hard enough it's calling right now, it knows your name.

## Susan Donnelly

FLASH MOB

At the sudden storm's height,
with its noise-battered screens,
rumbles and sputtering light,
while the rest of us watch

from inside, down the street
come the trash collectors,
singing, hallooing,
soaked past caring.

They hang on, jump off,
hoist, empty,
set back down again,
all the time shouting

and they don't look back,
when their truck moves on,
at the lightweights tipped
onto the sidewalk,

or the one that floats off
down the street-turned-river.

Isabelle Cartwright

## WHIRLS AND STINGS

Peter Denman, *Epigrammata: 64 Verse Miniatures* (Astrolabe Press, 2012), €15.
Edited by Chris Morash and Kevin Honan, *The Lighter Craft: Poems for Peter Denman* (Astrolabe Press, 2013), unpriced special edition.
Sheila Wingfield, *Poems* (Liberties Press, 2013), €14.99.
Emily Cullen, *In Between Angels and Animals* (Arlen House, 2013), €13.

'Witty, often paradoxical remark, concisely expressed' is the *Collins Dictionary* definition of epigram, and so is 'short, pungent, often satirical poem'; and Denman's verses are both. In sixty-four poems, one for every year of his life when this was published in 2012, the poet gives us classical Greece and modern Ireland. The poems about sex and death and everything in between, are pithy, among them a favourite, 'Leda':

> Bold Jove, intent to try it on
> With Leda, morphed into a swan;
> He knew it took some neck to mount her
> On what was just their first encounter.

The poems re-work myth and ancient history and are interspersed with four 'Health Notes', which despite their promise of being a salve to the poet's preoccupation with death are themselves intimations of mortality. Take number 20:

> This life is fast and fleet,
> There is no turning back.
> I don't mind the one-way-street,
> But alas! the cul-de-sac.

Modern Ireland is represented by the caricature, Fixer, who has of late entered Irish mythology. In the 'Notes' we're told he's 'a composite from Ireland of the recent past'. Imagine all the sliminess of an Irish banker cum developer cum politician cum lobbyist; in short, a 'boyo', and you have Fixer. Eleven epigrams follow his progress. Finally,

> Fixer, who had his price for which he'd sell,
> Now stares out through the bar-code of a cell.

Numbers 36 and 49 nod their head to Yeats. 'Autograph Tree' strikes a more serious note:

Poets and playwrights – all and each
Inscribed, while visiting Coole Park,
Initials on the copper beech.

These days, to protect the bark
Its trunk is caged and out of reach.
No modern writer makes a mark.

For what they are, these little poems from Peter Denman are a delight. With photographs and prints by Kevin Honan, the book, an 8x8 inch square, stands out in my bookshelf all by itself.

On 10 October 2013 the great and the good gathered to celebrate Peter Denman's retirement from his long-held English Department post as lecturer at Maynooth University. His gift was this fine collection of poems by his friends edited by ex-colleague Dr Chris Morash (TCD) and illustrator Kevin Honan. Aptly titled and borrowing from Paula Meehan's poem, 'The Last Lesson', the poetry is elemental. Many poems situate themselves in the air, heavens, jet contrails and 'the earth from above'; appropriate, when amongst Peter's passions are gliding and astronomy.

There is earth, fire and water too. John F Deane says:

Burn my tongue, I pray, with a live coal

that words on fire and unexpected
might flare across the darkening spaces.
                                    – 'GENESIS-FEET'

But of course the title also refers to the craft of writing poetry. Enda Wyley's 'The News From Here' balances skilfully a day at the seaside where the greater world intrudes through social media and books, but where:

There are winkles to pluck,
bladderwrack balls to burst
and razor shells
to scrawl with on the sand,
before the tide comes in,
this day's three words: *We are Here.*

Bill Tinley, however, is in the Heinrich Böll cottage in Doogort, Achill, and he's trying to write poetry. Punctuating his efforts with more turf for the fire, Baxter's soup, and ...

> a red, risotto, Port Salut,
> Tea afterwards, and Christmas cake from home

... the poet, in seven accomplished ten-line rhyming stanzas, finally pours himself a double Tullamore and determines to:

> Set out the cards for solitaire and play.
> Tonight, at last, I'll work it out for sure.

All of these poems are offered in deep esteem and affection for Peter Denman. As Jo Slade writes in 'Twine':

> Hands weave together a plait of words
> a bird might find, entwine her nest,
> keep her warm in winter weather.

Sheila Beddington (1906-1992) is perhaps best known for marrying Pat Wingfield, heir to the Powerscourt Estate in Co Wicklow, and for being a female poet from Ireland's dwindling Ascendency Class. This compilation gathers poems from eight collections dating from 1938 to 1983. The poems are selected, edited and introduced by Lucy Collins of UCD, and there is a short foreword by Brendan Kennelly in which he says Wingfield's poetry ranges from poems that deal 'with whole cultures and peoples and histories, to brief poems which, because they are vividly presented pictures, are quite haunting'. Indeed some of the poems are imagistic in style and are startlingly modern:

WINTER

> The tree still bends over the lake,
> And I try to recall our love,
> Our love which had a thousand leaves.

Leaves are everywhere. They appear in a third of some sixty poems, some of which are excerpts from longer pieces. There are 'salt-bitten leaves', 'bilberries in leaf', 'a leafless grove', 'the tremor of small leaves'; and in 'Sparrow', a 'bookleaf'. Her 1964 collection is titled *The Leaves Darken*, and in 'Continuity', 'We're [...] brittle as curled-up leaves'. Leaves represent the cycle of life but as she herself ages, she fastens more on their dying and eventual collapse. In 'Common Wish' she writes:

> Love plays in the sun,
> Sickens, droops and is done.

> A spider's thread
>  Rolls up, bind up her dead.
>   There is too much
>  For us between a dockleaf's touch
>  And Saturn, which with frosty rings
>  In utter darkness whirls and stings.

The early poems, some of which were published in *Dublin Magazine* and *The Bell*, begin to display what Collins terms as Wingfield's 'attentive use of classical materials and the unflinching scrutiny of states of human transition'. The later work, however, which was written after her marriage failed, Powerscourt Estate was burnt down, and she is mostly domiciled in England, is rather stark and seems to suggest that in the modern world, universal experiences are to be found not with gods and heroes but in the particulars of everyday rural lives.

Other motifs seem important too. We have thirteen references to 'soul', and in several poems bones and shells are mentioned. The poems deal tirelessly with existential questions and search throughout history for meaning and constancy, but it seems what she finds instead is memory. In 'For My Dead Friends', one of her stronger poems, she writes:

> To ease it calls for metaphor.
> I'll take, then, for my own
> Hand, the Parthenon, that hollowness
> Above new Athens
>
> [...]
>
>        that shell
> Now flushed by haze, colour of asphodel –
> And pick it up, and hold it to my ear
> Whenever, privately, I wish to hear
> Its murmur celebrate
> Those whom I knew
> Who were both good and great.

Emily Cullen's poems begin as a mixed tribute to pregnancy and motherhood. Cullen, in her mid thirties and then living in Galway, is 'an insomnia queen'. In 'A Promenade' she asks 'do I still qualify / as a "woman of destiny"? / Or am I an invisible mother / pushing a buggy into the sea?' In 'Damned If You Do...', in her characteristic half-rhymes she writes:

I am literate in love; fluent in
fluids, weaning and nurture.
Time to throw away the primers.
My darling, you and I
will learn by trial and error.

There is much soul searching here but ultimately, in 'Embodiment', one
of the stronger poems of the collection, 'I am held by this intuition: /
love / free of all.condition.'

Cullen is a harpist and qualified teacher of the harp. Her poetic style
is lyrical, intelligent and confident and the poems are searching in a
sophisticated and detached way. For example, in 'Amaryllis' she writes
'The amaryllis amplify / how it feels to be loved by you / from the inside
out.' The next morning the poet touches the 'carmine red trefoils' and
remarks:

Soon they will be pendulous,
shedding one by one.
But I will remember
how they hold their elative heads
On a stark december morning;
their sturdy elegance
irradiating everything.

Cullen has since emigrated to Melbourne and some of these poems are
written abroad. She goes on to explore many subjects: love, exile,
technology, all in a worldwide context. She conjures Clarke, Kavanagh,
Thomas Davis and Flann O'Brien, but also Mandelstam and Rumi. The
poetry is erudite and far-reaching and, as the title suggests, it touches on
the whole created universe, as the Elizabethans understood it!

Jim Maguire

SURFACING

Like spirits entering a body, they enter the sea.
Two men encased in the formality

of a room they've been decorating.
All day stepping on each other's shadows

side-stepping the rows
of chess pieces, stacks of creamy earthenware.

Evening at last, and they're in freefall
through the salty trapdoors.

One man surfaces with a glazed stare.
Is he losing the shade of his own heart

or confused by what he thinks
is a vandalised cross on top of the dunes

but is actually the ladder lashed
to the roof of the van?

Beyond is the house of the poultry man.
It feels so distant now

with its silos glinting on the bare hill –
like someone at the end of a heavy night saying

you either relate to things in a flippant way
or *really* hold them up to the light.

It's not the grain of the embrasure that counts
when a room is pressed into parsing

an afterpain. A remark left hanging
that strips even the roost of bats in the attic

of its glamour. Acoustics are everything.
Just ask the holymen chanting or arguing

on the lid of the ditty box.
How a dropped brush exploding

throws into focus the chicken man
framed with his lady on the baby grand –

a gaze which says she knows what it's like
when the mate you're swimming with turns

and turbo-mows away from the shore.
And yet behind the cool

a bloom – as if she's drawing something new
and unknown out into the light.

Jim Maguire

NANNERL, WHO NEVER BECAME A COMPOSER, SEES THE SEA FOR THE
  FIRST TIME

    *Calais 1764, en route to London*

A thing that runs away and comes back,
not all it's cracked up to be.
Papa in his impresario coat saying we're too indoorsy.
Eyes closed, I want to know it through my ears.
But can an ocean really be a clavier
rattling on the roof of a coach? Papa, I need to compose.
*Not that again! Where do you get your notions?*
And what of Wolfie? Sick from travel
yet chipper enough to be tickled
by the pooping waves and farting foghorns –
does he see how alive he is in Papa's mind?
Alive as the seabird gone under to breathe again
the slow-world solitariness, a berth
in the husk, a desk, a skeleton sketch.

Beverley Bie Brahic

THE JAR OF APRICOTS

Oval like a mirror, Chardin's painting
depicts a sideboard cluttered with objects,
some almost transparent –
others stubbornly opaque.

The woman has stepped out for a moment,
to fetch the missing ingredient.
Or has she only stepped back?
The mystery of her absence is compounded

by the pair of wine glasses: one looks untouched
but behind it and darker
like a mirror image, its double has been drained;

and the teacups, white porcelain.
From the near one, coils of steam.
In the mirror – if there's a mirror – the second
            is clean.

Beverley Bie Brahic

THE GOOD WIFE

Odysseus, the story goes, took a long trip, from Ithaca to Ithaca.

And she stayed home weaving the tapestry of her fidelity.

She was never tempted – so they say – by apples, pomegranates, or
    other signs of woman's frailty.

Now it seems Odysseus is back. Once again Penelope demonstrates
    her resourcefulness.

Question: if she's so smart, why didn't she rid herself of the suitors?

It's the sort of question too literal children ask. *Why did Goldilocks?*
*Why didn't Snow White?*

And the parents say – *It's only a story, besides it's time to turn out the*
*light: it's late and we've got dishes to do.*

*

Even once he dispensed with the suitors,
showered and tossed his clothes in the wash,
Penelope feared a god
was hoodwinking her.

Odysseus seethes. 'Find me some bedding,'
he tells the old nurse, 'I'll sleep downstairs.'
'Make him up the bed he built,'
Penelope corrects;

'put it in the hall. Heap it with fleeces
and coverlets we weave on our looms.'
'What!' bleats Odysseus –
'the bedstead I carved

from an olive tree, whose silvery leaves
shook like a virgin on her wedding night –
did somebody cut
our marriage bed from its root?'

*

So it *is* Odysseus, Penelope thinks.
After all these years.
She will miss her suitors. She looks
at Odysseus, looks at her wools
tinted the tender green of leaves
that edge the vinestock in spring,
and the black of mildewy grapes
left after the pickers have passed: fermented,
almost wine.
What will she do, without her suitors?

*

Penelope looks at Odysseus; looks at her unfinished tapestry.

*Perhaps,* she thinks, *a touch more carmine in the upper corner.*

## Beverley Bie Brahic

### NEAR KNOSSOS, A BORROWED HOUSE

Over the party wall, voices
argue. There's the old man, the
young man, an ingénue's treble –
grizzled patriarch, downy boy
stained with a moustache, a girl
who is marriageable
some god has his eye on.

Day and night, it never stops.
No parting shot with its seal
of blood; no slammed door, feet
stomping off. Not even the long
interrupted silence of Amen, So-be-it.
I suppose they have been at it
for centuries
like gods and the mortals.

Siobhán Campbell

## SPIRITS, SATIRE AND SONG

Patricia Monaghan, *Sanctuary* (Salmon Poetry, 2013), €12.
John W Sexton, *The Offspring of the Moon* (Salmon Poetry, 2013), €12.
Donna Sørensen, *Dream Country* (New Island Books, 2013), €12.99.
Aubrey Malone, *Mature Student and Other Poems* (Lapwing Press, 2014), £10.

The very title of Patricia Monaghan's *Sanctuary* might appear to give a sense of what to expect of the content. This however is not just poetry that seeks out the sacramental but also work that tries to create a transformative moment within its careful attention to liminal spirituality. The poetic strategies work best when exactitude of naming is trusted to convey a sense of why things are important: 'spikes of montbretia, escaped geranium' ('A Garden Near the Sea'). Occasionally, there's a less sure poetic step taken when making verbal claims about beauty and hope but the poems which are quietly authoritative outweigh these moments. 'Keeping Vigil in Renvyle' ends with a vision of 'spirits rising from the bogs like steam', and this is earned through a build-up of imagery laced with yearning.

Invoking the presences of Gobnait, Brigit and Latiaran gives Monaghan the opportunity to re-work legends including that of Gobnait's vision of the nine white deer, or that relating why there's been no blacksmith in Cullen since the fateful compliment to Latiaran's legs. The stories are deftly re-woven with a lightness of touch and an economy of expression. The sense of the spirit-power of strong women pervades the book and will speak readily to readers open to the summoning of this kind of presence, one of the things that a poem can do. Occasionally, there's a psalm-like short piece tucked into this book where the simplicity of longing is managed so that it catches out even the more cynical reader. 'Evensong', for instance, uses spare couplets to end:

> we pray that light remembers us
> as we traverse the darkness.

With a liturgical structure, and sections titled 'Book of Hours' and 'Land Mass', this book is an investigation of the holiness of land and mountain, river and well. The physical sites of the poems are foregrounded, with the central plain and the west/southwest of Ireland juxtaposed against the Driftless area of Wisconsin, in and around the land- and water-scape of the upper Mississippi basin. There's a softly rendered undertone of eco-awareness and an insistence on noticing the 'ordinary' which is powerful in its overall effect. Sadly, the introduction by the poet's husband speaks of her untimely death in her beloved locale of Black Earth, Wisconsin, in 2012.

In *The Offspring of the Moon* by John W Sexton, there are spirits too, but of the maverick, mocking kind, the kind that take delight in making gnomic pronouncements which appear to be off-kilter but turn out to have psychological truth. The first section presents a sequence of abused sonnets which delight in their own invention. 'William Blake Sees the Head Lice in Spectres' lives up to its title, ending: 'with a tuning fork he grooms eccentricity'. 'Soft Furnishings' is a cracker of a cat poem, destined to appear in future anthologies, where it will link the feline forever with tax evasion. A paean to the biro and to László József Bíró, 'Inventor, 1899-1985' may be about the sonnet form itself, but this is characteristically combined with philosophical fun, inviting the reader to send up the whole enterprise of writing itself:

> Hungarian; four-thousand-eight-hundred-
> and-sixty-eighth entry in my diction-
> ary; dead; immortal in every pen;
> full, dried-up, re-filled again and again.

Sexton also allows the surreal to come into the service of satire, becoming politically engaged in works like 'On the Morning a President Ordered the Invasion of Iraq'. In this mood he is faced with the challenge of all who write the political poem – that of matching artistic intent to content – and he arguably displays less control of the line in certain of these pieces. However, it's because of these different moods that the reader of a Sexton poem needs to be awake. There's a brio about his sharp swerves of imagination and a muscular musicality to his line which is particularly in evidence here in the poems which double as song lyrics, including 'The City of Angels'. Sexton manages to leave the reader with several nuggets of expression which will draw one back to the book: the frog who is 'the Omega of swallowed things', the devilishly clever 'Tao of Earthworm' with its minnow 'anchored by a single prick'. In other work, Sexton plays more forcibly with form and language in the manner of a freewheeling Edwin Morgan and with the attitude that every poem is an experiment in tone and word. His book title may well be a nod to Morgan's 'The First Men on Mercury', but even if the link is not intentional, these two poets share a dynamic understanding of the performative nature of a poem, in how it comes off the page and creates an after-presence.

In *Dream Country*, Donna Sørenson works with a kind of heightened sensitivity in poems which clearly stem from deeply felt emotion. At times, there could be more control of the latter. Lines such as 'and I am doomed to thrash my life away // just to keep breathing' feel less resolved than in other instances where an image is created from lived incident: 'She went inside, splashed ink / all over her clothes / and wrote about her lovers / and lost children' ('The Individual Qualities of Cloud'). As hinted at by the title, these poems are peppered with references to dreams, to sleep, to slipping out of consciousness, to dusk, to the dark, to waking, to souls and to death. There may be an attempt in the opening poems here to set up a dichotomy between the 'two worlds' as mentioned in 'Penumbra' ('you lie between two worlds'), but this section of the work is so committed to one of these worlds that the other doesn't get a look in. The more successful poems leave that dream country to one side and, as in 'The Pilgrimage', instead explore something that the poem does not know before being written, an innocence of intent which can successfully generate a memorable image, such as the 'slapping hand of light upon the girl / shocked her into life'. There's a theme of 'home' running through the work and a poem to that very notion called 'An Idea of Home'. Sørenson might re-consider William Carlos Williams's 'no ideas but in things' to see if instead of finding a simile for home, there's a way of beginning from the objective, allowing that to seed an aesthetic moment which could combine rootedness and its constant loss in one.

Elsewhere, scenes from domestic life become freighted with the emotional economies of care as in 'Knives, Forks and Fathers' and here, as in other poems where actuality trumps dream, there's a chance for what is at stake to acquire real consequence. This is work driven by a palpable depth of feeling and the latter is matched best when specificities of image and scene are used. I will remember the woman who's 'Mortality was on top of her' as she fully registers 'the dried wine stains' of her life.

*Mature Student and Other Poems* by Aubrey Malone is a book brimming with the personality of the author. It begins with a compelling narrative piece titled 'Alma Mater' based on the rhythm of the spoken sentence and presented in tight four-line stanzas. A note of wry nostalgia tempered with ongoing unease is set up here and corroborated later in several other poems. The temporarily uplifting presence of screen heroes and the momentary glamour of cinematic stories from outside the narrow-minded island which is the speaker's home are tropes that run through this work. There's a critique of what the poet calls 'our lazy selves' and a sense in poems like 'Old Haunts' of time lost to platitudes, 'like the spools of a film / you've seen one too many times before'. The poet uses what may seem like rather old-fashioned rhetorical devices including posing questions, addressing the reader directly, and using the second person in poems where it may not be warranted. At times, the poems become framed as a kind of intellectual battleground with the self.

Violence and the potential for same is never far from the surface, and the short piece 'Fugitive' could be a coda for the whole work, where the reach for an almost dishevelled gothic seems a reaction to an apathy around societal and political lying:

> A street-sign sighs in the wind
> Here, where the murders lurk.

The 'tinker-child' who enters the poem and whose face is 'wet with the transience / of decades' turns out to be disarming in more ways than one. Malone is keen that the poem be the site of tensions such as those between youth and age, between the idea of 'feminist' and the actuality of a constrained life, between those who think they know better and those who take to the drink. The presence of mental illness and of recovery is another subject treated here, one which fits with the clear-eyed realism and anti-romantic nature of this poet's voice. Interspersed between the (mainly) narrative poems are two other kinds. One is a short lyric which reaches for a symbolic register as in 'Farmer', where 'The dead entrails of all lives / come back to haunt us', and 'The heather is blazing / but the hills are dead'. The other is concerned with taking a tonally inventive position in the service of a gentle satirical humour, as in 'They Also Serve', which is both a list poem and an extended conceit where the waiter who asks 'Is everything all right?' is given an answer far beyond the one he would have wanted. At over 100 pages, this book could have been edited to eliminate some unevenness but overall there's a distinctive atmosphere to the work.

These are four very different voices and as far from 'the usual suspects' in terms of poetry emanating from Irish publishers as you are likely to find. Three of the writers are well-served by their publishers in terms of attention to the page, though the two books from Salmon Poetry (Monaghan and Sexton) are the most pleasing as objects, followed by the Sørensen published by New Island, where the sans serif typeface is less easy on the eye. The Lapwing publication by Malone would have benefit-ted from extra leading between the lines and one hopes that Lapwing might receive some public arts funding to improve upon their covers. That being said, it's a pleasure to encounter the range of expression here, four distinct answers to 'what is the poem for?'

# Andrew Fitzsimons

## PEACE AND NOTHINGNESS

Thomas Kinsella, *Late Poems* (Carcanet Press, 2013), £9.95.

Thomas Kinsella's *Late Poems* is a book of culmination, of last things, and of first things looked at again in the light of age. It collects the five most recent of Kinsella's Peppercanister series: *Marginal Economy* (2006), *Man of War* (2007), *Belief and Unbelief* (2007), *Fat Master* (2011), and *Love Joy Peace* (2011). As with the earlier Peppercanisters, each of these separate volumes contains a thematically interrelated sequence. There are poems in each of the sequences that do what Kinsella has already done, which re-articulate a dogged commitment to art, and to the messy business of living, but there is a new sense of almost intimidating authority, and of refinement of purpose:

> That the life-form as we have it
> is inadequate in itself; but that
> having discovered the compensatory devices
>
> of Love and the creative and religious imaginations
> we should gather in each generation
> all the good we can from the past,
>
> add our own best and,
> advancing in our turn
>                  outward into the dark,
>
> leave to those behind us,
> with Acts of Hope and Encouragement,
> a growing total of Good (adequately recorded),
>
> the Arts and the Sciences,
> with their abstractions and techniques
> – all of positive human endeavour –
>
> in a flexible and elaborating
> time-resisting fabric
> of practical and moral beauty …
>              – 'BLOOD OF THE INNOCENT'

This is a book of unapologetic high seriousness. 'First Night' returns to the beginnings of Kinsella's art, to the 1950s and to the window of the flat in central Dublin that was the setting for that great early poem, 'Baggot Street Deserta', where adult life, and poetry as a major component in that life, began to happen: 'My brain at the window, / absorbing a new view of the world.' Kinsella's language over the nearly sixty years since 'Baggot Street Deserta' has, as is well known, rinsed itself of rhyme and traditional rhythms. What is less appreciated is how, at times in this later work, Kinsella's language has turned to a lyric utterance that both mimics, and is a commentary on, prayer:

> And remember that My ways
> that can seem in the short term
> mysterious and unfair
> and punishing to the innocent
>
> will justify in the end
> the seeker after justice
> and not the power seeker
> crumpled in his corner.
> — 'ADDENDUM'

*Marginal Economy* contains one of Kinsella's greatest poems, early or late, 'Marcus Aurelius', which combines a Cavafy-like portrait of the world of the Emperor-philosopher with an introductory section of late-Kinsella at his most gnomic, and Joycean:

> Gaspbegotten. In shockfuss.
>     Out of nowhere.

The brilliance of the poem lies in its distillation of the historical material, the way in which that material mischievously echoes affairs closer to home ('Threatened on the Northern border by brutal tribes / with no settled homes') and, ultimately, its completely achieved tone of 'baffled humaneness':

> Called upon for decisive positive action,
> at which he was more than averagely effective;
> but preferring to spend his time in abstract inquiry,
> for which he was essentially ungifted;
>
> he kept a private journal, in Greek, for which
> he is best remembered. Almost certainly
> because it engaged so much of the baffled humane
> in him, in his Imperial predicament ...

What is remarkable in these late poems is that Kinsella's concerns are not so much with the decay of body and the death of friends, but with how things began, and began, invariably, to go wrong. There is little explicitly Irish material here; the range is vast: there are echoes of the Dead Sea Scrolls, the Psalms, Job, the *Iliad,* we move from the 'beliefs of the first Church' to entomology; the perspective is uniquely Kinsella's, removed and involved, a clear-eyed accounting of the 'irresistible / . . . movement and nature of things'. There are poems here, it has to be said, which retain the privacy of dream, but whose details form part of a concern with routine and ritual, with attenuated forms of ceremony, and with the transfiguration of vital experience: 'the courtesies formed themselves / under their otherworldly burden / into the first outline of a sacrament' ('Love Joy Peace'). There is also, unusually for Kinsella, a commissioned poem. The epigraph to *Man of War* reads: 'On being asked to sign an appeal for the abolition of war'. Yeats, when asked for a war poem, reacted by offering what Edna Longley has called an 'anti-war-poem war poem'. Kinsella takes a different route. As circumspect as Yeats about the commission, he drains it to the dregs for its bitter and brutal ironies, offers a Swiftian proposal to end war, and takes the opportunity for some self-mocking humour:

> I would be even willing to assist
> with my own first proposal; arbitrating
> in cases of dispute at mortal chess.
>
> Not with the hangings or decapitations
> – I hate the sight of blood. A mere injection
> leaves me uneasy for a while.

*Late Poems* nods towards Yeats in its title, but its nominated masters reside among 'the orders of earthly genius': Bach (Fat Master), Michelangelo (the epigraph to the book quotes his Sonnet XI, 'Where nature simply made, you understand') and Ben Jonson's 'mortal Beloved / ... *that must sweat to write a living line*'. The final poem, 'Love Joy Peace', sweeps through the history of the early Church, the Reformation, Christian teachings on the workings of grace, toward a final statement of artistic faith, all prompted by the memory of the eponymous graffito, painted everywhere by persons unknown around the 'first neighbourhood':

> Joy of the flesh.
>
> Saying all it can of love.
>
> Peace and nothingness of the last end.

David Cooke

FALLING

> *Exodus 7: 8-12*

Year by year the portents came,
telling us nothing we wanted
to hear: at times calamitous,
yet stirring, more often,
despondent pools.

On stylish plazas, where the augurs
touted reasons, they played
a game called Sticks and Snakes
as blether reached the skies –
trying to guess the clouds' secrets

when all they knew was birds
falling. A shift at the poles –
it makes sense and may be possible.
In the end it left us shaken
to see them scattered everywhere

on our lawns and driveways:
their flitting eyes switched off;
their feathers, dulled and stiffening,
become as pointless
as a dowager's fan.

Simon West

THE TAKING UP OF WORLDLY PURSUITS

Once, from in a spell that courage worked
on us we spoke of sailing, for the world
was fluent as the sea. Now I look back
with longing and it seems in truth we yearned,
like Augustine, to use names as a glue
and found a universal hierarchy.
Do you remember when Emilia
tugged at the corner of your untucked shirt
saying, 'Hey, careful your soul doesn't float up to heaven
without you!'? You laughed in agreement,
but later woke in a cold sweat,
wanting everything to be itself.

If I compare that phase of my life to a stream,
fast-moving and marred by eddies where the water
churns around a flaw, reflecting little
of sky or shore, am I guilty of artifice?
Each day I swim in the ocean and dig the roots
of seedlings into pots. Only now
as I climb without rest up and down my ladder
do I begin to learn how each of us
must be put to the test of likening.

## Ocean Vuong

(STANZA BREAK)

The tide has swallowed his legs
& I am swinging open
the passenger door. I am running
toward the horizon's shut eye,
running out of a country
to run out of. I am chasing a man
the way the dead chase after

days. The way each grinning wave chases
its own shatter. I am running. I am
already here: a wet stillness
in my father's arms. & although
I can no longer hear it, I can tell,
by the way his neck tilts
as if broken, that he is singing
my favourite song.

Hannah Jansen

LESSON IN GRIEF AT CONEY ISLAND

We bought Nathan's hot dogs,
drank beer from yellow cups,

walked a shard-strewn beach
and an ash-dark dock.

We swung in the cage
of the Wonder Wheel

over merry-go-rounds stitched with light –
pinwheels, drink umbrellas –

while the night pitched ceaseless tunes
onto bejewelled blue horses,

the great, rough mirror of the bay.
On the Cyclone, we lurched.

The machine sent us up
before the first drop:

the track's wooden vertebrae,
hipbones rattled and slammed.

We felt everything
and nothing. Didn't know

which to prefer – deafening descent,
bodies thrown forward into the dark,

insides balled into themselves,
or the stillness that came before.

## Anna Woodford

FACIAL

Softly painted by Fra Angelico,
as if by angels, are disembodied
hands on a wall of a monk's cell
in Florence that halo the holy face
– as it waits between blows –
with sticks and stones. That room
floats into my mind as the other

side of this one where I lie
like a little god, having stumbled
in after work. The air is full
of oils, and her hands
hover in the sacred space above
my prickled skin – touching me
just before they touch me again.

Lesley Harrison

MIRROR MIRROR

She knew this woman like a sister:
recognised her eye, her smooth chin
and lip line, turned to an angle,
caught in the clouded silver rim

like a pool of dark, still water
absorbing, a gradual subtraction
until she was her own thin reflection
intriguing, almost uncoloured

and then one day, walking in the forest
she met herself coming back, alone
(full fleshed, a little older)
bare headed in the august rain
stepping past, nodding.

# Lesley Harrison

## NORTH : BIRDS

### SNIPE

It sprouts from the ground, rasping against stones and reeds like dry
rain, or wind, or autumn. The soft organs are tucked away in a small
pouch near the heart. It lays down growth rings, like a tree.

### EIDER

A clean bird, well woven. It finds a hole in the water, and waits,
crooning its undersong. A pot of feathers.

### GOLDEN PLOVER

A clear wind; a water eye. A warm breath above the ground. A dip of
mottled eggs.

### BARNACLE GOOSE

A necklace of blue-black shells, all pendicle and mouthing, like
seaweeds attaching to timber, their hard beards filtering the tide.

### SNOWY OWL

Their eyes are beetled. They are lupine, furred. They fly up to the
outer air, white fading into white, seeding the clouds with snow.

### PTARMIGAN

Their pinions are wind-sharpened. They roost on a sun-warmed
stone. In summer they rattle the grass above the tree line. Their
young have cowls of lichen.

### IVORY GULL

It is mute, like a pearl. It holds its own dull gleam, like a lamp in
winter rooms. It feeds on light alone.

Philip Cummins

## GOD IN THE UNIVERSE

Elaine Feeney, *The Radio Was Gospel* (Salmon Poetry, 2013), €12.
Susan Millar DuMars, *The God Thing* (Salmon Poetry, 2013), €12.
Micheal O'Siadhail, *Collected Poems* (Bloodaxe Books, 2013), £20.

The poems collected in Elaine Feeney's *The Radio Was Gospel* boast a maturity in tone, voice and scope; where 'The engine was missing' in 'The Red Tractor' from 2010's *Where's Katie?*, Feeney's latest collection probes *why* the engine is missing:

> You hail de Valera's constitution,
> fantastic parchment inscribed
> with the right wing of God.
>     – 'FOR THE NUNS, FOR THE NUNS'

> A liberties woman
> sent begging letters
> from her tenement table.
>     – 'BEGGING LETTERS, 1913'

Dedicated to her mother and grandmothers, Feeney's collection examines motherhood in poems such as 'Mornings' and 'Birdsong', and explores what it was to be a mother for previous generations in poems such as 'Pity the Mothers' and 'Dublin Town', while 'Birdsong' also shares a sense of literary awakenings:

> The gentle mother showers books
> to her daughters' eager hands.

Set during a time when 'The battle guns haven't / touched the sweet ditches / of the young Republic', the enriched, refined register of 'Birdsong' provides a generational contrast with 'Dublin Town'. In the eighth stanza of the latter poem, the poet breaks free of the maternal spirit that pervades her experience on the city streets, instead indulging in the literary interests and contemporary concerns that will later define her work:

> I am alone in the Martello Tower
> in nineteen-ninety-nine
> whoring myself to Joyce and the apocalypse.

It's a refreshing dynamic within just one of the many 'list' poems collected in *The Radio Was Gospel* that don't, however, 'sing' so much as shout. 'Mass', 'Drowning', 'Boy' and half-a-dozen or so other poems that contain stanzaic lists might resonate strongly on stage, though they're too didactic to retain any longevity on the page and, gradually, begin to wear a reader down.

Also, lack of tight, rigorous editing hampers the collection: clunky lines ('But all of us were and none of us were / and children can smell that love and lies', from 'The Radio Was Gospel'), and misleading layout ('Junior Infants' ends, seemingly, mid-sentence and with a gaping space towards the foot of the page, only to be continued on the following page), work against the poet's progress, as does poor placement of poems. For example, two excellent poems, 'Child' and 'War', both austere, subtle poems of celebration and grief, respectively, would carry more impact had they been placed on adjacent pages.

If Feeney's poems, such as 'For The Nuns, For The Nuns' and 'Mass', cover religion from a historical and sociological perspective, Susan Millar DuMars's *The God Thing* – dedicated to her late mother-in-law, Mary Higgins – finds a poet who identifies as agnostic in the title poem ('God, I wish I could believe. // Help me. / Feed this hunger'), and who asks the bigger questions – unapologetically so – in language that is direct and immediate: 'You mock me for searching / for God in people. / Even if I don't find Him / what better way to love them?' ('Leaving Ponder's End').

Many of the poems in *The God Thing* are energised by kinesthetic imagery, placing an emphasis on the present, the living: 'I offer my arm, but that isn't / what she wants to hold onto' ('Harm'); '[She] pushes beans around her plate. / I push words around / this page. Both have gone cold' ('Near the End').

Similarly, DuMars's ekphrastic poems on Henri Matisse and Edward Hopper – a perennial favourite amongst poets – both seek, as ekphrastic poems do, to give a work of art a second life. Inevitably, such poems also tend to reflect on the artistic process itself. The most successful ekphrastic poem in *The God Thing* is the exquisite 'The First Blue Nude', which features Lydia Delectorskaya, a muse and model of Matisse's who cared for the then wheelchair-bound artist until his death. It is difficult not to read the following lines ...

> She indulged
> the man who could not stand
> inside the frame but only
> to one side, looking

... and not recall Flaubert's description of the ideal author, in a letter to his mistress, Madame Louise Colet: 'An author in his book must be like

God in the universe, present everywhere and visible nowhere.' The influence of confessional poets such as Sexton and Plath throughout *The God Thing* means, of course, that DuMars *is* present everywhere. Indeed, it feels from DuMars's depiction of Lydia and Matisse in the lines above that DuMars sympathises with Matisse: Matisse cannot 'stand / inside the frame' and capture a portrait of both himself and his muse within the same frame; by contrast, DuMars celebrates the fact that she and her muse, that is, her late mother-in-law, are both captured within intimate lyrics across many of the poems collected in *The God Thing*.

There are missteps: a central simile in 'Learning to Swim' – 'like teaching / a toddler to stand. Thus we shuffle along' – doesn't advance on Shakespeare's 'an old man is twice a child', while the glib tone and jaunty lines of 'They Put Down Ronan's Neighbour's Dog' ('Not "put down", *killed*, / that's how Ronan says it / *killed him. Great fucking dog*'), no doubt an attempt at light relief, feel out of place next to poems such as 'What I Most Recall about the Funeral', 'Matisse Near the End' and 'The God Thing'.

The book finishes, however, on the excellent 'This is How You Say Goodbye', where the 'yellow rose' that 'sighs / as it lands on the coffin lid' in the opening lines picks up the 'yellow-grey ghost in too-big pyjamas' in the opening line of the first poem, 'Harm'; a nuanced end to a multifaceted collection.

Like *The Radio Was Gospel* and *The God Thing*, Micheal O'Siadhail's *Collected Poems* is dedicated to a woman: the poet's late wife and muse of 43 years, Bríd, who died prior to the 2013 publication of O'Siadhail's *Collected Poems*. While O'Siadhail's 2005 collection *Love Life* might well contain some of the poet's most uncharacteristically confessional poems, such as 'Ceremony', 'Selves' and 'Parkinson's', O'Siadhail's poetic fascination with women began in 1978 with 'Motion of Thanks', the opening poem from his debut collection, *Leap Year*. 'Motion of Thanks' is an ode 'To that delightful woman, / Who gave to Micheal one year's pension / To sit on a bench in Stephen's Green'. O'Siadhail concludes that 'This indolence it was that shaped me. / All rights reserved', echoing the poet's decision in 1987 to resign his professorship at Dublin Institute for Advanced Studies and devote himself to writing, full-time. This decision also coincided with a shift towards collections that focus on entire themes, such as the Holocaust (*The Gossamer Wall*), love and friendship (*Love Life*), globalisation (*Globe*) and, in perhaps O'Siadhail's finest single collection to date, his experience and training as a linguist (*Tongues*).

The best poems in *Tongues* deliver on O'Siadhail's claim in the collection's foreword that 'Languages have infinite ways of looking at the same thing.' In 'Mother', motherhood is entwined with etymology, bridging the relationship between the nurturing and evolution of a child and the origin and development of language:

*Mère, madre, mare, maire* or *madro*
How we'd guess that mater was the source
But since we all come from Latin know it's so.

That poem's opening line ('Whenever I think of snow I think of her') is echoed in 'Snows', the poem adjacent to 'Mother': 'Snow. Our Indo-European word, / Sniff and snivel noun of crystal flakes, / Sneaking manna blizzard, / Soundless whirlings over our cradle place.'

Not only does 'manna' pick up 'nanna' from 'Lullaby', the poem previous to 'Mother', but it also echoes 'mamma', which O'Siadhail uses in the poem 'Friend', suggesting that the poet's writing on the theme of interconnectivity in *Globe* took on a poetic and linguistic power for him in *Tongues*.

Just as Joyce and Plath influence the work of Feeney and DuMars, respectively, Donne is very much a conscious and, at times, companionable influence on O'Siadhail:

> Great Leveller. Azrael. Lord Pluto.
> La Faucheuse. Sweeping and grand.
> Was Donne right? *Thou art so.*
> — 'ONE'

> Young transgressions are flings of bliss
> Beside such nursed or bitter umbrages,
> The brooded resentments of old age.
> That, Donne knew, was the real abyss.
> — 'DREAD'

> Everywhere becomes everyplace.
> No man is an island Donne knew
> Before the instant image wheel
>
> Relayed the tube's mute appeal.
> — 'SPUTNIK'

Kavanagh also looms large for this deeply spiritual poet. Just as DuMars's *The God Thing* takes Beckett's line that 'All Poetry is Prayer' as its epigraph, O'Siadhail's *Collected Poems* carries through all of its 828 pages Kavanagh's claim that 'a poet is a theologian'. O'Siadhail's intellectual curiosity about the ways we live our lives is continually evolving; he writes in *Globe*'s 'Shift' of 'The way a word's meaning shifts', and of how 'All generations face up to this / Slippage of what's familiar'; a mark of his alertness to change and eagerness to engage with a contemporary reader.

Justin Quinn

CRITICAL GRATITUDE

Jody Allen Randolph, *Eavan Boland* (Cork University Press, 2014), hb €49.

Eavan Boland – as a poet, critic, teacher and activist – has played an integral role since the 1970s in transforming the status of Irish women (as well as of Irish men). Her friendship with Mary Robinson is particularly iconic in this respect – their spheres of action complemented each other, as they helped change the country, legislating both a new politics and a new imagination. In her introduction, Jody Allen Randolph remarks that 'Boland's work can be seen as part of a process in which, through witness, protest, narrative and autobiography, the lives of women became a necessary critique of Irish culture.' The only inaccuracy here is in the words 'can be seen' – they should be replaced by 'is'.

   Allen Randolph has worked closely with Boland over the years, and her book profits from this, above all in her extensive quotations from an unpublished memoir. But proximity also brings its dangers for a critic. One symptom is the way her critical terms harmonise with Boland's own, and her reluctance to interrogate the poet's story of her emergence. A key idea here is what Boland variously refers to as 'the national poem', 'the closed models of Irish lyric poems' and finally the 'toxic lyric'. This poem seems to be rhymed and patriotically deploy a simplistic nationalist iconography. Boland often couples her resistance to its politics with her abandonment of traditional technique in favour of more open forms.

   But where is such poetry in the twentieth century? Although there is much rhymed poetry to be found, from Yeats to Mahon, this work is sophisticated in how it approaches Irish topics. Neither is it in MacNeice, Clarke's mature work, nor Patrick Kavanagh. (You might find it in the work of lesser lights of the Revival, which Clarke's early work belongs to, but they're of little relevance). The generation of Thomas Kinsella, John Montague and Richard Murphy, which immediately preceded Boland, again offers no clear examples that might fit her narrative. Moreover, these poets – especially Kinsella and Montague in works such as *Nightwalker and Other Poems* (1968) and *The Rough Field* (1972) – were the first important figures to use modernist technique when approaching national themes. While they were by no means radical experimenters, their formal choices put Boland's in perspective (she often figures her rejection of rhymed and metred poetry as more dramatic that it was – in one interview she refers to herself as a kind of 'dissident' in poetic terms). The suspicion grows that this 'national poem' is merely a straw man for the young, female, solitary poet to take apart. The only poet who might possibly have ever written it is Thomas Davis.

That Boland repeatedly overstates her own achievement does not mean she has achieved nothing. Poets and artists continually indulge in such narratives of struggle about themselves and their successes. But criticism does well to judge such claims at a distance. Boland's stature is by now canonical and she no longer needs critics who will defend her from the cheap, lazy sniping she endured in Ireland during the 1980s. Her claims require the complication of a more nuanced critical debate. The best passages here provide this, especially where Allen Randolph looks at Boland's involvement in Northern Ireland, both as a young journalist and, more obliquely, in her anthology of German poetry. Also important is the way she situates Boland in the Irish women's movement of the 1970s. Uninterested in the pub culture of literary Dublin, she found a different community at Gaj's Restaurant, with Robinson, June Levine, Mary Kenny and others. This would confirm her in the new direction her poetry was taking. Another signal achievement is the book's coverage of family history. Boland has made clear how important her mother was to her own artistic development, and there are few surprises here. Allen Randolph marks eddies in her relationship with her father, complicated by his position as an important figure in the new Republic (above all, as President of the General Assembly of the United Nations, in which func-tion he faced Nikita Khrushchev banging his shoe on the desk), as well as the fact that his family ran a workhouse for half a century, till it was closed in 1924. In contrast with her childhood, her time in Trinity and feminist activism, Boland's tenure in Stanford University from 1996 seems more of a victory lap than a source of further change in either her poetic development or feminist outlook. But who knows what will emerge in the future?

The Stanford period also coincides with a certain repetition and exhaustion in Boland, which Allen Randolph, try as she might, cannot but register. When the study deals with these books – from *The Lost Land* (1998) on – we come across comments about how this or that poem 'draws together many of the themes of Boland's previous books', 'encompasses many previous themes', is a 'return to a motif familiar in her prose as well as her poetry', 'revisits two of her now familiar themes', 'explores a theme consistent in Boland's earlier work', 'brings a new resonance to some of Boland's now familiar questions'. Part of Boland's dramatic effectiveness has been achieved as a result of the spectacular endurance and consistency of her critique. But a collateral consequence has been the imaginative monotony of many of the later poems.

Boland has substantial critics, among them, Denis Donoghue, Edna Longley, David Wheatley, Brian Henry and Caitríona O'Reilly. Apart from a passing mention of Longley, we only hear about lesser figures from the 1980s, among them Mark Hutcheson, Douglas Sealy and John Jordan. (The ill-judged remarks of the last three are aired by Allen Randolph, and that was enough to refute them). But a study like this would have been an ideal occasion to deal at length with, say, Wheatley's critique of Boland's representation of Gaelic culture, or Longley's argument that the 'nation' Boland speaks of in her work is oversimplified, unable to take into account events in Northern Ireland (despite the attempts noted above). Many of these criticisms have yet to be answered by Boland's advocates. (On a different level, it's a pity the book did not have a further round of proofreading).

Grand claims can be made for Boland, and Allen Randolph substantiates many of them with critical insight and accuracy. The Czech Republic, where I have lived for the last two decades, has no one with the same international visibility, critical energy and polemical abilities. While there was a strong feminist movement in the 1920s and 1930s, these were erased by the successive waves of Nazism and Communism, and almost three decades since the Velvet Revolution, Czech literature still only has a patchy awareness of the importance of gender in literature, let alone in politics. Thus, as we search fruitlessly for the 'toxic lyric', disagree with her depiction of the Irish language, and wish that her idea of the nation was more complex and closer to reality, we can be grateful to Boland for making feminism so central to debate in Ireland.

# Hugh O'Donnell

TO MY SISTER IN FAVERSHAM

How are they now, I want to ask,
the limes at the foot of the hill,
all arthritic knees and elbows,
ten or twelve of them in the dip
by the redbrick asylum for the aged
whose families have reduced them
to a handbag clutched on a lap,
a postcard from some sunny part.

There must have been a wall,
some estate posing for attention
behind these remnant sentinels,
gone careless now, as you stride
past early mornings, Bramble
straining ahead for the wood
that no longer exists, rousing
the ghost of a scent he might chase.

## Geraldine Mitchell

HOW THE BODY REMEMBERS

Last night I was woken by a loose scrap of siren
and found you, face pressed to the night,
watching some drama unfold on our road,
cobalt strobing the silence

the way it lit up the street that September
in Trastevere, washed over you blue after blue
where you lay among fag ends and chair legs
until they lifted you onto a stretcher

and breath guttered back through your lungs
as we lunged over cobbles in a language
unknown to us and you found yourself
back in a nine-year-old body

careening through London's cacophony
of sirens, bomb flares through blue glass,
the City in flames, your eyes wide
with terror and me holding your hand.

# Jordie Albiston

## IT

it is pure    that last gentle breath    &
applied    quite gently to death    I hold your
face in my palm    tell you thank you for all
those difficult sums    say thank you for adding me up    your eyes go still in Rilke's
*open*    that space    & thank you for times &
for plus    you never minused you never
took away    were one of those Platonic
solids & here in my hand polyhed-
ral love in the shape of a perfect shape

       you are pure    & applied to life    Euclid's
       dog to the last    I don't shake I don't shake
       you but how can I go on    it is all
       mathematics you would say just chuck the
       ball    see it isocline to sun    chase down
       any blacknesses    when you're happy run

Patrick Maddock

DISTANCES

at whatever hour it was
in the early darkness
when the flash occurred
sudden and intimate
as if inside my eyelids

I'd already forgotten
the difference between
the speed of light
and the speed of sound

but in the not-knowing
I softened the experience
of counting out the seconds

by distracting myself
imagining two people
indistinctly featured
in a bed such as ours
on the far side of the hill

where the one that was for me
leaned over you as other
and waited just beyond
the rumble of the thunder
to offer you his answer

Jonathan Ellis

ANOTHER GLASS OF WATER

Edited by Conor O'Callaghan, *The Wake Forest Series of Irish Poetry* (Vol. III): Colette Bryce, Justin Quinn, John McAuliffe, Maurice Riordan, and Gerard Fanning (Wake Forest University Press, 2013), $19.95.

Anthologies of poetry can be miscellaneous affairs, dependent all too often (for good and for ill) on the interests, tastes and whims of their editors. As Anthony Howell recently observed in a wonderfully acerbic survey of Britain's anthologising culture for *The Fortnightly Review*: 'Categorisation defeats the purpose of any anthology ... A good critic knows that rather than plumping for a specific school one should seek out extremists in a diversity of directions.' Seamus Heaney and Ted Hughes clearly followed this methodology when calling their first anthology together *The Rattle Bag* (1982). 'This anthology amassed itself like a cairn', they claimed. 'Most of the poems lay about for the taking in places already well known to people, younger or older, who read verse; only a few came from the by-ways. They were picked up one by one and left *in situ* without much initial thought being given to the stuff already in the pile or the position they might occupy in the final shape.' Heaney and Hughes were clever in their evocation of natural selection here. Although a cairn, like an anthology of poetry, is organic and man-made, subject to random choices and decisions but shaped ultimately by human hands, they emphasise the organic, pretending that the poems selected were simply there 'for the taking ... only a few came from the by-ways'.

Conor O'Callaghan, in his brisk introduction to Wake Forest University Press's latest selection of five Irish poets, is equally upfront about the arbitrariness of his anthology-making. His poetry-cairn is, if anything, even more carefree than Hughes and Heaney's, without quite going as far as Howell's gathering of 'extremists'. According to O'Callaghan, the work 'happened in a two-decade period from the early 1990s onwards'. But what happened and to whom? O'Callaghan discusses what happened to Ireland during this time and the consequences of this happening on the poets who were born there but now live mostly elsewhere. Yet, as he admits, 'The only real connections between these poets and their work are their Irishness, their mutual inclusion in this book and the fact that four of five have made their homes outside Ireland.' Having written this, he does go on to risk a more formal grouping: 'If the poets here are collectively indicative of any one thing in Irish poetry, it is of a reaction that occurred gradually towards greater formal determinism, a more international perspective, empiricism, rationalism and wit.' How do we make any kind of grouping or school out of such openly defined qualities? O'Callaghan goes out of his way to prevent us doing so. Happenings don't tend to last long in the memory. They are performance pieces rather than play texts, things that live in the here and now rather than the forever after. It is difficult to review most anthologies without objecting to what has been left in or out, what measures up to scrutiny and what lets us down. But that doesn't appear to be in the spirit of anthologies like this one that wear their happenstance quality so very much on their sleeve.

The five poets that O'Callaghan anthologises are all very good. I probably like two poets much more than the other three. Of the two poets I prefer, I certainly have favourite poems. When I began as a poetry reviewer for *Metre* almost 15 years ago, I would have spent the remainder of the review defending these prejudices. Thinking about contemporary literature today, I have become more circumspect of such strong opinions, particularly where poetry is concerned. I keep remembering what Elizabeth Bishop (no fan of anthologies, particularly those featuring only women) once said: 'I'm not a critic. Critics can't rest easy until they have put poets in descending orders of merit; they change their lists every night before they go to bed. A poet doesn't have to be consistent.' What I admire most about this anthology is its inconsistency, its refusal to be one thing. I love the imperfections that every poet reveals. Their good and bad days.

I was captivated, for example, by Colette Bryce's interest in lines and tenses. Days after reading her poem, 'Satellite', I am still haunted by the image of her father emptying coins 'from the money-drawer of the pub / where he'd spent the night before / pulling pints for the late drinkers'. The 'errant dime or quarter' that makes its way home over the Atlantic is an apt if troubling image for the Irish diaspora. Do Irish-Americans still feel a responsibility to send money back to their homeland? Maurice Riordan's Hitchcock-inspired, 'Time Out', is just as memorable. A scruffy lone parent pops out to buy some cigarettes once his children are asleep. Knocked over by a 'U-turning cab' in the second stanza and pronounced dead on arrival at the hospital, we are brought back to the house to see what happens when the children wake up. The two children end in a heap at the bottom of the stairs before finding the TV remote. At half past nine, the 'screaming begins'. It's like the shower scene in *Psycho*. Yet magically, and unnervingly, Riordan begins the poem again. 'Let us get *this* dad in and out of the shop, safely across the street, / Safely indoors again'. This feels like a Hollywood ending, but one so self-conscious we are forced to consider our own addiction to certain storylines. Should a poetic ending always be a tragic one?

In the interview that prefaces each selection, Bryce reflects on the important business of composing poems by hand: 'For me, poetry doesn't get written in straight lines, or from the top of a page to the bottom. It definitely gets written in little explosions, or clusters. I think if I were to write straight into Word for Windows, the poems might end up as predictable as the format implies.' One of the many delights of the book is the accidental disagreements between poets, accidental because we only feel them to be disagreements by reading the anthology as a whole. Whereas Bryce rejects composing on a screen, Riordan sounds more like a recent convert. 'The screen is a great reusable canvas', he enthuses. 'Sonnets and villanelles are ideal "page" poems. I doubt I could have written "The Sloe" on paper – unless I was using a toilet roll!' Gerard Fanning is the most fun interviewee. There's an aphoristic quality reminiscent of Philip Larkin about many of his replies. When asked about the difficulty of love poems, for instance, Fanning refuses to say the word 'love': 'If I'm celebrating anything, it's the joy of persistence.'

These interviews between editor and poet are always illuminating, even when the two fail to see eye to eye. I particularly enjoyed Justin Quinn's response to O'Callaghan's question about form. 'Did these forms happen organically, or were they part of a formalist conviction?' he asks. 'That's a tough one', Quinn replies, before rejecting the very basis of the question he has just been asked:

> For me this question doesn't really apply to any art. Take a dancer for instance: one doesn't ask a dancer if he's able to do what he does organically, spontaneously. Or a painter. Artists and writers can reach a point where they wield the hard-won technique naturally, like a dancer. The form becomes a mode of thought, not a mould for it. A way of measuring breath and cadence. Which is a way of life, and a trajectory of emotion and sensibility.

The poems that follow this statement emphasise Quinn's care for form as 'a way of life', delicate but never attention-seeking. I love the relatively early poem, 'Highlights', in which the sonnet form divides two couples, much as a thin floorboard separates us from our neighbours. In the octet, the couple downstairs overhear the couple upstairs, all 'tirades and injured feelings'. The sonnet turn could have been used to depict the couple upstairs as louder and perhaps more in touch with their feelings than the couple downstairs voyeuristically listening in. But Quinn's turn is more circumspect, less obvious. The second couple certainly make less noise than the first – is that why they are given fewer lines in the poem? – but their inner lives are no less dramatic. The difference between them is 'what goes on between, in silence'.

John McAuliffe's work is also characterised by interference and interruption. He is particularly astute on the difficulty of being neighbourly. In 'Moving In', for example, he reflects on how much ground to concede to one's neighbours when they prefer things as they were before you moved in, not as you want them to be. McAuliffe, like Quinn, resists the tendency to reminisce. His memories of childhood are nearly always memories of 'going places, / Telephone wires on either side, like fences / For giant invisible horses'.

The one poet that I cannot place, that baffles me more than any other, is Gerard Fanning. I don't think this is a question of awkwardness or allusiveness, though the poems have elements of each. Rather it is something to do with an utter uniqueness of tone that I cannot compare to any other poet I have read. At first I thought this was only present in the shorter poems, but on reflection I think it is equally true of the longer sequences as well. Here as an example is the very short poem, 'She Scratches His Wrist':

> She scratches his wrist once or twice
> They tell in signals of their private vice.
>
> I am a witness, not some eye from above
> Some things we do not know, or only tell in love.

I annotated my copy of the book with the following questions: Who scratches whose wrist? What 'private vice' is communicated between them? Is the 'I' in the second stanza different from the 'she' and 'he' of the first stanza? Is the 'eye from above' God, or an allusion to a private eye? What 'things' do we 'not know' and how does being 'in love' change matters? Why are the first and third lines without punctuation when they seem to require at least a comma? Why does this poem get under my skin? What scratches at my wrist when I read it?

I couldn't help smiling at Fanning's reply on being asked how he writes poems: 'My efforts are more like the child past bedtime, insisting on yet another glass of water.' This is true of the overall effect of reading this anthology. For all that one learns from five very different poets, one doesn't feel exhausted or overwhelmed on reaching the end of the book. On the contrary, like a child at bedtime, I wanted at least one more poem.

Gearóid Denvir

RÍORDÁINESQUE

Ed. by Frank Sewell, Seán Ó Ríordáin: *Selected Poems* (Yale University
Press, in association with Cló Iar-Chonnacht, 2014), €19.99.

Seán Ó Ríordáin is, without doubt, the most important poet to write in
Irish in the twentieth century. Indeed, it could be argued that his is the
most significant poetic voice in the Irish language since Aogán Ó
Raithille in the eighteenth century or even Dáibhí Ó Bruadair a century
earlier. As with Ó Bruadair, his work was a *nuachruth*, an innovative move
away from an earlier tradition, though still firmly grounded in that tradition. Ó Ríordáin, as can be seen not only in his poetry from the outset,
but also in the recently published extracts from his diaries, *Anamlón Bliana
ó Dhialanna an Ríordánaigh* (Cló Iar-Chonnacht, 2014) edited by Tadhg Ó
Dúshláine, was intensely conscious throughout his life of the fact that he
was creating something new. He mentions again and again that he was
saying the previously unsaid, thinking the previously unthought in his
work, and that he was changing the very meaning of the term *filíocht*
within the Irish tradition. In the earlier tradition *filíocht* was a narrative of
the communal, but Ó Ríordáin aligned himself in his work with the
modernist understanding of the function of poetry, at the core of which
is the over-riding importance of the voice of the individual poet.

Readers of Irish poetry are, of course, aware of the importance of
the work of Ó Ríordáin and of his rightful place in the poetic hierarchy
of this island. However, readers of poetry in English in this country, and
indeed worldwide, are for the most part unaware of Ó Ríordáin as no
significant body of his work has been readily available to them until now
in that language. While the editor of the present volume admits that
'There is simply no substitution for reading Ó Ríordáin's poems in the
language of their composition', the publication of this beautifully
produced, dual language *Selected Poems* of Seán Ó Ríordáin ensures that a
substantial body of his work is now accessible to the wider world. In
addition, Sewell's perceptive introductory essay provides both an
overview of the scope of Ó Ríordáin's poetry and an outline of the literary,
cultural, linguistic and intellectual contexts from which the poetry
emanated.

The list of translators reads like a Who's Who of Irish letters. Some,
like Colm Breathnach and Celia de Fréine, are among the foremost poets
writing in Irish today. Others, like Paddy Bushe, Frank Sewell and Robert
Welch (*Grásta air!*), have published both in Irish and in English, while

others still, like Ciaran Carson, Theo Dorgan, Paul Muldoon and Mary O'Donoghue, are significant poets writing in English but with an intimate knowledge of poetry in Irish. The editor, Frank Sewell, has selected well. Perhaps one might argue about his choice of certain poems over others – the present reader would argue strongly, for example, for the inclusion of the seminal long poem 'Na hÓinmhidí' from Ó Ríordáin's ground-breaking first collection, *Eireaball Spideoige* (1952). One might even quibble about the translations of certain words or lines. However, the end result is that the poetic voice of Seán Ó Ríordáin is well presented by his peers to the global English-speaking world.

If the art of translation is no simple matter, and if the art of translating poetry is especially difficult, the work of Ó Ríordáin might be taken as a particularly apt case-study. Ó Ríordáin created throughout his poetry what he himself might have described as a private language (*teanga phríobháideach*) in order to 'syllabicate' his particular read of the world in which he found himself. His use of newly created compound words, often combining the concrete with the abstract (e.g., *scillingsmaointe* = 'shilling thoughts' from the poem 'Saoirse' / 'Freedom'), or his creation of a verb from a noun (e.g., *do shiollaib sí* = 'she syllabicated' from the poem 'Siollabadh' / 'Syllabication'), not to mention his many flights of linguistic and poetic fancy, present particular difficulties to a translator. One can translate the word, but it is far more difficult to re-interpret the world, to arrive in translation at what Ó Ríordáin would have called the level of *fo-intinn*, the subconscious mind of the poem.

That being said, many of the translations in this volume actually make that creative leap and do justice to the original Irish poems almost as poems in English in their own right. Colm Breathnach beautifully recreates the rhythm and tone of both 'A Sheanfhilí, Múinidh Dom Glao' ('Old Poets, Teach Me the Call') and 'Mo Bhás Féin' ('My Own Death'), as does Paddy Bushe with the whimsical 'Cláirseach Shean na nGnáthrud' ('The Venerable Harp of the Mundane'). Celia de Fréine reproduces most skillfully the rhythm, the musicality and the playfulness of 'Cuireadh' ('Invitation'), and Mary O'Donoghue's rendering of 'An Cat' ('The Cat') is a triumph of translation. She not only captures the metre and tone but also succeeds in 'riordanising' the original (*ríordánú* being the term the poet himself coins in his poem 'Tost' / 'Silence', to describe his own creative process), right down to the creation of a Ríordáinesque compound, 'cat-heart', in translating 'Is sceon i gcroí chaitín' as 'its little cat-heart afright'. Frank Sewell achieves a similar success with his beautiful rendering of one of Ó Ríordáin's most iconic poems, 'Na Blascaodaí' ('The Blaskets') which resonates with the musicality and the *fo-intinn* of the original as Ó Ríordáin would have intended.

Unfortunately, not all the translations are as felicitous as the aforementioned. The translation of 'Oileán agus Oileán Eile' ('This

Island and the Other Island'), one of a series of important long poems of religious doubt from *Eireaball Spideoige*, loses its way at times and does not reflect the hesitant effort at a Kierkegaardian leap of faith which permeates the original poem. In this context, 'Dazzlement or some devil / holds me under a spell' does not really do justice to 'Bíodh dalladh nó diabhal / Am shiabhradh'. Moreover, 'you went romping' fails to echo the sensuous, sexual overtones of 'do rincis-se go macnasach'. Furthermore, 'do thusa ceart', which is a key phrase in any critical reading of the poem, might be better rendered as 'your true self', or even as 'your real self' or 'your inner self', if one wished to avoid what might be seen as a cliché in English, rather than as the rather colourless 'the right you'. Another canonical Ó Ríordáin poem, 'Fill Arís' ('Return Again') also falls prey to the translator's difficulty in finding the *mot juste* for some of the key concepts of the poem: 'éirim', for example, is more than just 'intellect' in the original, and the words to express one of the underlying ideas not just in this poem but in all of Ó Ríordáin's poetry, the quest for 'an cló ceart', which is the climax of the poem, is weakly rendered as 'your right shape'.

Interestingly enough, Ó Ríordáin's own translations of his own poems are prosaic, literal and sluggish, 'prós in áit na filíochta', 'prose instead of poetry', as he himself says of what he terms a failed poem in 'An Peaca' ('The Sin'). His translation of 'Cúl an Tí' ('The Back of the House') lacks the frolicsome gaiety, the innocent lack of guile and the childlike magic of the original. As for the well-known 'Saoirse' ('Freedom'), Ó Ríordáin's translation is almost verbatim, remaining over-faithful word by word to the original, and thus losing the poetry in the translation. Paul Muldoon's translation of the same poem on the other hand is a typical Muldoonesque poetic recreation of the original, much in the same way that he translates, for example, the poetry of Nuala Ní Dhomhnaill, even if he 'leaves out' some of the 'factual detail' of the original.

All in all, this volume of translations of the poetry of Seán Ó Ríordáin does justice to the original work, and will help establish the importance of Ó Ríordáin in the pantheon of Irish poetic voices for those who do not read Irish, and should be required reading for anybody with an interest in twentieth-century Irish literature, culture and social history.

# Séamus Barra Ó Súilleabháin

SIAMSAÍOCHT

níl aithne agam ar an bpáiste ionam
dá mbeadh aithne agam air
do thréigfinn é i gcarrchlós Disneyland
in aois a naoi mblian dó,
i dtreo is go ngabhfadh an garda é
is go bhfaigheadh an créatúr
laethanta saoire shíoraí
in Ifreann na nÓg
bheadh a rogha aghaidh fidle ar a cheann
togha na milseán ina phóca

is AK47 ina ghlac.

# Séamus Barra Ó Súilleabháin

GUÍ

> *Níl aon ní is géire ná mallacht baintrí nó guí file*
>    – seanfhocal


scrios ar chóras
scrios ar anord
scrios ar dheis
scrios ar chlé
scrios ar shaorstát
scrios ar thuaisceart
scrios ar fhál
scrios ar dháil
scrios ar ghaeltacht
scrios ar dheontas
scrios ar chraos
scrios ar chléir
scrios ar chruinneas
scrios ar shaibhreas
scrios ar dhiabhail
scrios ar dhia
scrios ar **loit**ríocht
scrios ar an dán seo
scrios ar 'mise'
scrios ar 'tusa'
scrios ar chéitinn
scrios ar raiméis
scrios ar stair
scrios ar chromail
scrios ar ár
scrios ar dhúchas
scrios ar oiliúint
scrios ar fhaisean
scrios ar shean-nós
scrios ar phóit
scrios ar raithneach
scrios ar oideachas
scrios ar an oireachtas
scrios ar airgead

scrios ar ór
scrios ar méféineachas
agus scrios

ar gach scriostóir.

féach,
tá gach rud scriosta.

Deirdre Doherty

HUMMINGBIRD

Though it's impossible, I see, to take back what's already been said,
you're still dead, a hummingbird hasn't returned with no poem in its
beak yet, last night I took off again. Every turn in my sweat stained
bed robbing the planet of angular momentum, I flew backwards, in
reverse time lapse, like a hummingbird in ultra-fast motion. Below
my white wings, chapel chimneys sucking up smoke; demolished
warehouses rushed back up; that bright white lily pad blooming into
a huge hot air balloon. Soon, planes lassoed back into their runways,
the pop up antennae, green telephone boxes, writing unwritten on
blackboards, sand dunes unretreating, egg yolks unbeaten – you. You
back blasted – you smiling at me – before you jumped from your still
swinging swing. It makes no sense to us. In my best dreams, before I
wake going over my regrets – what I said – in a prison that did not
then exist, the whistle & click is the sound of your mother pouring
tea as if I flew back where I'd already been, unuttered the key.

# Deirdre Doherty

JOHN'S POEM / FRAGMENT

So, I'm past the notion of 'fragments of you existing beyond the final beat of your heart, the death of your brain'. I could tell it would be big. The wood panelled frame would exceed 80 x 26 inches. People would pass. And though they wouldn't see your hippy hair – how fucking gorgeous you were – they'd get a glimpse of that triumphant grin blooming like a yellow flower against a long black background. Your words then merely gathering momentum – freshly crashing through my head – soon hurtling on, beyond just one friend you'd encounter. Reader, they die. And that, you'd think, would be the end of it? But you too will continue to make an impact on the world in real, measurable, ways, beyond the idea of a soul, beyond the immortal breath or, as I said, the despairing human brain which first created it.

Deirdre Doherty

DEAR JOHN

But worse, now that you ask, for a soldier. She'd laughed, of course,
at the dog tags, black jokes, trench art. At cards, she'd throw again,
keep the Ace, her voice rising when he holds his cock her way.
Twelve months in; blindfolded, knee deep in blood, the voice braves
the shells, whirr of planes overhead, the next near blast. At night: his
talk of running, a quick death, the pain, drowned out by an octave.
And no volta, no turn. Shell-shocked, lungs burned, so cold a man's
warm word could kill, she checks her six, copies that. In. Out.
Breathe. Speak. Welcome Home. And yeah, perhaps no Dear John?
Proof of it? With a letter you could at least fight the noise, see your
own voice reach a vanishing point

# Gerard Smyth

THANKSGIVING
 *– in memory of Michael Smith*

About his life, the facts are in order
but the poet is missing and an elegy is called for
or at least a thanksgiving
for his book of dedications,
his days when he listened to a schoolroom clock
that seemed slower than time,
slower than the narrative of Caesar's wars,
a journey to the village of stone and dust
where they still had Good Friday Crucifixions
and the hired musicians played all night
the flamenco songs of Andalusia.

The poet is missing – has he gone
to Machado's garden or Mangan's doss house?
Perhaps to blend with the colours of the Alhambra,
seek again the after-rain stillness
of the air out west in Connemara.
No – he is gone the hidden ways
close to the river mouth where his song began
in the clamour of the bird market,
whistle of the North Wall Dredger Man.

Gerard Smyth

MISSISSIPPI

The local river carries its name from one end
to the other, from the lake in the north to the delta
in the south; passing through the land of God

the first stranger it meets is the devil
learning to swim, plunging in
but keeping away from the Christening pool.

Sometimes it turns to mud in the muddy creek
or breaks loose to seek the Governor's
Mansion on the way to Baton Rouge.

In its waters there are bones, there is blood.
There are towns that need it
and towns it washes away in a punishing flood.

Little has changed since the slave looked at it
and saw freedom; since an image of the river
was painted to hang in the county museum.

The local river knows the lonely despair of the loner
and the light of transfiguration, light that shows
the poverty of trees when they are out of season.

Judy Brown

PRAISE POEM FOR THE URBANITES

Too soon I felt the loss of the city. The pull
of its mass – all of you clustered there – held me.
I was drawn out of true by the physical drag

of what I have to call *longing*, here in the open:
a countryside plugged with delicate stony towns,
hamlets kept apart by nothing but space.

Where you are, lights twitch in the air.
An unnatural fur clings to the back of the fridge.
Your balconies leave me no room to run

but from the church green, where I hang
under the sound of bells, I can feel you all stir –
oh my cellmates! – in a proximate sleep I've never left.

I take a stroll at dawn to the flooded quarry.
The whole fucking time I think of you dancing,
electrics fizzing in your brains a handspan apart.

I'd take it back: life as a farmed salmon, oily
with antibiotics and omega 3, abraded fins
wafting in over-cooked water. Or, the press

of bodies in a tankful of harvestable muscle.
I want this: the shift of skin's anonymous touch,
the warmth on the other side of the wall.

Gerald Dawe

A KIND OF SURRENDER

Mark Strand, *Collected Poems* (Alfred A Knopf, 2014), $30.

> 'When I read poetry, I want to feel myself suddenly larger ... in touch
> with – or at least close to – what I deem magical, astonishing. I want to
> experience a kind of wonderment.'
> – Interview with Wallace Shawn, *The Paris Review*

Mark Strand, one time US Poet Laureate and Pulitzer Prize-winning
poet, died last year at the age of 80. He was, according to Dan Chiasson
in *The New Yorker*, 'a great poet and a kind man'. Quite likely, along with
poets Philip Levine, Carolyn Kizer and Galway Kinnell who also died last
year, he was little known outside of the poetry circuit on this side of the
Atlantic, although Strand was well acknowledged within the States.
Alongside fellow poets of his generation with whom he shared aesthetic,
professional and personal connections such as Donald Justice and
Charles Simic, Strand taught throughout his life at numerous colleges in
the States, giving public readings from the early Sixties as well as
maintaining a longstanding, practical devotion to the visual arts, poetry
in translation and editing numerous poetry anthologies, such as the
essential *The Making of a Poem*, edited with Eavan Boland (2001).

In one of his books on art and artists, his little masterpiece on
Edward Hopper (*Hopper*, 1994), Strand remarked:

> When I was a child what I saw of the world beyond my immediate
> neighbourhood I saw from the backseat of my parents' car. It was a
> world glimpsed in passing. It was still. It had its own life and did not
> know or care that I happened by at a particular time. Like the world of
> Hopper's paintings, it did not return my gaze.

Something of this childlike vision characterises Strand's poetry. Along
with the stillness, there is an almost Beckettian silence at its heart.
Strand's pure, lightly idiomatic English, shedding the vernacular energies
of American social life as much as the eager resourcefulness of its speech,
has at its root a steely poise; almost a chilly calm. In his collection *The
Late Hour* (1978), there is a poem, 'For Jessica, My Daughter' – poignant
to recall, it was in her New York apartment where Strand would die last
November – in which the characteristics of Strand's inner landscape are
in place:

Afraid of the dark
in which we drift or vanish altogether,
I imagine a light
that would not let us stray too far apart,
a secret moon or mirror,
a sheet of paper,
something you could carry
in the dark when I am away.

Light and dark, the revolving constellations of sky, the fleeting journeys in various settings – American, primarily but also other countries, other cultures, especially Latin American – and the influence of Wallace Stevens are present from Strand's earliest collections, including *Sleeping with One Eye Open* (1964) and *Darker* (1970).

There are prose experiments such as the last single volume he produced, *Almost Invisible* (2012). There are also extended poetic narratives (*The Monument*, 1978), story-telling as in the book-length *Dark Harbor* (1993), and modern fables as in *Blizzard of One* (1998). All are gathered into the five hundred and ten austerely printed pages of Strand's challenging *Collected Poems*.

For one so productive, it is strange to read that at various times in his life Strand gave up writing poems and turned to making his own art (for instance, his impressive collages), rigorously refusing to repeat himself and seeking instead to find a bridge through to another kind of poem. If this didn't happen he seems to have had the moral courage to wait. Indeed there is a sense of waiting in the writing itself, as in Strand's sense of poetry in general. In one of the valuable interviews he gave throughout his writing life – well worth checking out – he said some fascinating things about his own ideas on making poetry.

'A poem has its dignity, after all', he remarks in a conversation with Wallace Shawn published in *The Paris Review*: 'I mean, a poem shouldn't beg you to read it; it's pathetic, if that's the case.' That sense of the separate reality of the poem, of it being like a state of mind, detached from the efforts of the poet, brings in a further note which sounds quite counter-cultural today: '[P]oems not only demand patience, they demand a kind of surrender. You must give yourself up to them.'

Very early in life, Strand left Canada and travelled with his parents wherever his father's job took him throughout the USA. They settled in no one place for long, so it seems. In his poetry, there is a sense of estranged yet beguiling fascination with space, rather than with the particularities of place, that might well have a root in that childhood transience. As in the poem dedicated to Elizabeth Bishop, 'The House in French Village':

I would sit
with my grandmother,
my aunt, and my mother,

the four of us rocking
on chairs, watching
the narrow dirt road
for a sign
of the black

baby Austin
my father would drive
to town and back.
But the weather
was not often clear

and all we could see
were sheets of cold rain
sweeping this way and that ... '

The reader can't help feeling that the diction of Strand's immaculate
poems – the cool deracinated sense of observing ways of life to which
one does not fully belong, and never can – brings to the work a structure
of regret as much as an unflinching eye on the wider frame, as in 'For
Her':

Let it be anywhere
on any night you wish,
in your room that is empty and dark

or down the street
or at those dim frontiers
you barely see, barely dream of.

Strand's *Collected Poems* is a singular achievement; it has all the concentrated
focus of a truly distinctive art of wonder.

# George Szirtes

RAGS AND RICHES

Tom Paulin, *New Selected Poems* (Faber and Faber, 2014), £14.99.
Ciaran Carson, *From Elsewhere* (The Gallery Press, 2014), €13.90.
Louis de Paor, *The Brindled Cat and The Nightingale's Tongue* (Bloodaxe Books / Cló Iar-Chonnacht, 2014) €15.

This frail, frayed, rich, tangled fabric – more rag than fabric – of language has to clothe us all. Out of it we may weave what we can, patching as patch can. There are patching techniques available in poetry of course: the cento, the collage, macaronic verse, and more. Macaronic is particularly interesting in that it deploys a variety of languages, one of the best known most glorious examples of it in English being John Skelton's *Spcke, Parott*, where the parrot in question declares:

> Yn Latyn, in Ebrue, and in Caldee,
> In Greke tong Parott can bothe speke and sey,
> As Percius, that poete, dothe reporte of me,
> *Quis expeduit psitaco suum Chyre?*

Adding, elsewhere:

> So many morall maters, and so lytell usyd;
> So myche newe makyng, and so madd tyme spente;
> So myche translacion in to Englyshe confused ...

Tom Paulin's early poetry was characterised by a plain-spoken, flinty social realism with a strong moral sense. 'My loathsome uncle chews his rasher'; 'tenants of the room / Chew rinsed lettuce and watch the street'; 'Something made a fuck of things'; 'that slumped smell / From the blackened gasworks'. If we wanted to describe Paulin as a self-consciously dour writer we could rest our case there but would be pulled up by 'slumped smell'. The language here springs to attention, fresh as grass. The poetry is less in the plain language of social realism, more in the springing, in the coiled resilience of the sudden foreignness of 'slumped'.

Among the austerities of an argumentative or narrative lyric such sallies of linguistic high spirits seem like small explosions. In a later poem, 'The Sting', the ostensible subject of which is the sensation of being hit in the eye by a wasp, Paulin shifts into hyperdrive, writing 'it resembles that moment / when the windshield binges / into quartzy toffee'. The voluptuousness and eroticism of a poem that turns out to be about passion and pain proceed from there.

There is in the later Paulin a constant and ever more urgent seeking for the colours of the raw. At its freest, as in the longer autobiographical 'The Wind Dog', the search becomes an intoxicated adventure. In the course of it Paulin discovers a book called *The Hamely Tongue* and fixes on the word 'jum', meaning 'a large, unreliable trouble-giving car'; one he watches ...

> bob over the sheugh to Broagh
> to the riverbroo
> the mudshelf of the bank

... going on to ...

> and wee Louis in the room above
> hearing the brangle of talk
> rising through the floorboards
>
> o chitterin chatterin platinum licht

There is something odd about this 'hamely tongue' in that it depends on a colloquial that the poet himself presumably does not use in conversation, the whole forming a kind of cento, an invention, a parrot-speke patched from languages exoticised by way of authenticity.

In the same poem Paulin talks about the opposite of 'that brangle of talk' which is, in his own mischievous terms, an 'echt British' that claims to be a genuine language:

> except that's always fake somehow
> it's machinery means of production
> not a spring well
> – the well of Anglish
> or the well of Oirish undefiled

Here is another plea for authenticity but one that is more troubling: the defiled well is, after all, a classic racist trope. We may be sure that Paulin doesn't mean it that way – I am sure there is not a racist bone in his body – but this definition depends on an idea of the pure based on birthright. One should not poison wells, of course. One should be pure bred, pure water, pure well with full access to echt Anglish and Oirish.

There is, according to this instinct, a distinction between an 'authentic' speech with proper roots and a defiled and bland machine speak, or rather between Paulin's interpretation of the authentic as a macaronic tongue involving the several oralities of *Speke, Parott* and a computer-addled Google Translate. The closer to the physical mouth the better for Paulin.

The cover of Ciaran Carson's *From Elsewhere* declares only one author, in other words a single mouth, but there are two, the other mouth belonging to Jean Follain, a generous selection of whose poems, translated by Carson, forms half of the book. The translations appear on the verso, Carson's own poems, responding to each of Follain's translated poems, on the recto. Carson, in his introduction, regards translation as a 'fetch' or apparition, 'a shadowy counterpart'. Ironically enough, the only thing missing is Follain's original French, the thing that casts the shadow and produces the fetch. We are in a game of shadows and re-mouthings.

Follain died in 1971 at the age of sixty-eight. For an anglophone reader his translated poems resemble those of his better known friend and contemporary Eugène Guillevic in their brevity and avoidance of metaphor. There is nothing of grandeur in them, no rhetoric of any kind: the voice is straight and plain, keeping close to the ground. This much is clear from Carson's exciting and persuasive translations, their own language plain yet subtle, beautifully pitched.

'Page franchie', rendered as 'A Page Ventured', consists of only seven lines. We see a sheet of paper in an office, a half-eaten loaf of bread next to it, note the time, then, in the last three lines, remark how

> a minuscule insect utterly alive
> vibrates, ventures forth reddish-brown
> across the written page.

It seems little enough, hardly more than an Imagist jotting, but the process – the perspective – is much larger. From one angle it is Bede's sparrow spurting across the hall, from another it is a tiny rough beast slouching towards an altogether different future. The fact that Follain manages this leap in scale and time with such power is in itself remarkable, but it is Carson who is managing it for us. In a later poem, we slip from whales to the dropping of a pin, and in 'Le globe' / 'The Globe' from the image of a schoolboy carrying a globe to his schoolmaster to 'the wine sinking / down the gullets of the blacksmiths / in their dogskin aprons'.

Carson's own poems are good, as they could hardly fail to be given Carson's ear and intelligence, but most of the time their clear derivation from the original puts them in the shade, as genuinely 'shadowy counter-parts'. I can see why the poems were written in answer to the originals' inviting gesture but Carson is at his best when he lets go, not only of the theme, but the model itself, leaving only the process as in one of his major successes, 'The Hunters', where the meeting of two wives, two husbands and two ships conjure gunfire and foghorns and a sudden freshness that is normally so characteristic of Ciaran Carson's poetry.

Louis de Paor is new to me, chiefly because his published work has been in Irish and not published in the UK. His translators in *The Brindled Cat* include Kevin Anderson, Biddy Jenkinson and Mary O'Donoghue, though the book doesn't tell us who did what, but the English versions – however arrived at – carry the power of genuine oral performance. There is nothing tricksy about the language but there is a great deal of narrative play and wit. The imagery is taken from common life as observed at first hand mostly, but transformed by a delight in resemblance and transformation. We see this in an early poem like 'Long Horns', where 'light in short pants / runs barefoot in the garden', and in the later 'Pride of bearing', where we find the shape 'that best becomes you / your belly great as the minster bell / sounding the irregular hours'.

These appear to be incidental delights but there is a Chagallian inclusiveness and generosity in the poems that is more than its incidents. The poetry can turn to darkness and the public world as well as to the intimate village or street, as in the beautiful 'Silk of the kine', 'when flight EI 32 / turned its dipping snout / towards home', and in the affectionate, humorous, yet meticulous bringing together of colonialism and its attendant theoretical language with a crowd at Shannon Airport. I am so pleased de Paor is in an English that, as he says in his Introduction, enables him to read the translations of his poems 'as if they were my own, rather than a script prepared by others'.

Skelton's Parrot is the brilliant speaking shadow of plain talk. Through translation the world of plain talk is re-experienced as freshness. Paulin's solid realism has all the authentic feathers of an exotic bird. In Carson's Follain and in the translations of de Paor, voices talk back plainly enough but come to us fresh.

# Liam Ó Muirthile

OUT THE BACK
  – after 'Cúl an Tí', by Seán Ó Ríordáin

Tír na nÓg is out the back,
A wonder-topsy-turvydom;
The Fourlegged Gang strut about
With no shirt on, in their bare-ahs,
With no Taw Shays or How'r'y'-ahs?

But every bare-back out the back
Is covered in hurly-burlydom;
Aesop, the *Cúl* Dude, understood
The long-ago lingo they yap,
but he's long gone out the gap.

Flocks and chicks peck out the back
With stumpy *Moody Blues* the duck,
Jet the *Black Dog* is a mean cur
Who snarls and curls and growls,
And *Sunny* the cat purrs out milky vowels.

The heap of trash out the back
Is a world's wonder of treasure;
A candlestick, buckles, an old straw hat,
A groovy mouth-harp in mute metal
And a snow-white goose-necked kettle.

Tinkers hollering out the back
'God Bless You's' and 'Holy Molies';
They meet their own clan out the back
Panhandling with open hand
At each backdoor in Ireland.

I'd like to be out the back
At all hours in the dark,
To meet on his moonbeam rounds
Professoreen Aesop, the sprite,
Our *Cúl* Dude and erudite.

## Stephen Connolly

ANOTHER EXCHANGE

The heavy door was open. I was a sinner,
a simple country person, the least of all believers,
but something of his boyish face was easing

from the off. His boyish face that flickered
in relief against the wall, his boyish hands
sleek as polished glass. Music played allegro

as the moon made its slow advance through
the skylight across the floor where as instructed
I placed a turnip at his feet whereupon his sleek

boyish hands and quick boyish tongue were moved
to act, his voice becoming my voice, his hands
becoming my hands as he carved from the turnip

my father the deacon's face. He told me what I had
to hear and I was quick to mention war, whereupon
his boyish eyes receded far beyond the night.

I was about sixteen at the time.

# Ciarán O'Rourke

THE PRISONER
 *– photograph of Keith Douglas*

The photographer
has shot too soon,
so you'll stand

like this forever:
unappeased
and reticent,

your uniform heat-
creased, eyes widened
for the rain

that may fall daily there
to burn a thrumming life
to dust.

Finding you this way,
opened onto
on a page your diffidence defies,

the past becomes
what later
knowledge lacks,

the fact
before the story
of the fact, perhaps,

or the watch-strap
tightened
on a boyish wrist,

and the man
not checking it
as the camera strikes.

And yet, to look again,
there is space, too, behind
your fierce unreadiness

for softness
to unfold itself; enough
even for the poet

to stir in this image
of soldier, son, and lover still,
and show

which verve of air
and coolness out of earth
were yours that day,

and which our own
in the imprecise
perfections of the past

we wreak. Wanting you
so remembered, I feel
that I could wait

a thousand hours
for your gun-dark gaze
to clamber

out of the stifled light
you're wrapped inside,
and blink un-

photographed,
near with words,
on the heat-forgiven sand …

A fly enters the room
in which these wishes writhe,
lights on the hand

that would grip time's net
like this, and shake you
out of it, lithe with life.

For an instant, history
is an insect, caressing skin,
and what poetry there was

vanishes, in which you'd lift
your frantic cigarette
to mouth, and speak.

Learning from your reticence,
I know
that when this creature

escapes the brittle cage
of my attention
I may return

to press the living weight
of breath
impossibly through air

until your
almost poetic
poet self walks free ...

Though, as I look
from your unmoving
portrait now,

it seems that being true
to that half-gentle, grim-
lipped glance you give,

I must note with care
this fly that squats
so curiously

on the slope
of my wrist –
yes, and try

to replicate
the immense, inhuman
watchfulness

in its tiny poise,
its eyes and fingers
beautifully unfearful

of what my bone-
dull hand conveys:
a stillness

total as your picture's is,
but riddled also
with heat

in the mind, the sun-
caught suddenness there,
and the blood-beats.

## Dermot Healy

THE PLOUGH

The new plough in the sky
has moved to the sea side
of the house

to dig a white furrow
through the long acres of clouds
and star nests in the sky.

The old plough of the earth
has come to rest
at the gable,

to question the heavens,
with feet
and ribcage gone skeletal.

There the symbol sits rusting
under its new coat of blue
while the shape it once threw

moves on
along the lazy beds of the constellations,
like a letter in an old alphabet

whose sound is lost
to the tongue;
till, at daybreak, the work of the metaphor

is done.

– from *The Travels of Sorrow* (The Gallery Press, 2015)

# Notes on Contributors

**James Aitchison** has published five collections of poetry, including *Foraging: New and Selected Poems* (Worple Press, 2009). Rodopi Editions published his *New Guide to Poetry and Poetics* in 2013, and will publish his critical study, *Madness, Sanity and Salvation: The Poetry of Anne Sexton*, in 2016.

**Jordie Albiston** has published eight poetry collections. Her work has won many awards, including the 2010 New South Wales Premier's Prize.

**Beverley Bie Brahic**'s poetry collection, *White Sheets* (CB Editions, 2012), was a finalist for the 2013 Forward Prize. Her translation, *Apollinaire: The Little Auto*, was awarded the Scott Moncrieff Prize earlier this year. Her most recent translation is *Yves Bonnefoy: The Present Hour* (Seagull Books, 2013).

**Judy Brown**'s *Loudness* is published by Seren Books (2011) and was shortlisted for the Forward and Fenton Aldeburgh first collection prizes. She has been poet-in-residence at the Wordsworth Trust at Dove Cottage in Cumbria (2013) and writer-in-residence at Gladstone's Library, Flintshire (2014).

**Siobhán Campbell** is Associate Professor in English Literature and Creative Writing at Kingston University, London. Her books include *Cross Talk* (Seren, 2010) and *That Water Speaks In Tongues* (winner of the Templar Poetry Award and shortlisted for the Michael Marks Award). She is the editor of *Courage and Strength: Stories and Poems by Combat Stress Veterans* (Kingston University Press / Combat Stress UK, 2012).

**Isabelle Cartwright** has written poems, interviews with poets and poetry reviews for *Poetry Ireland Review*, *The Irish Review* and her own literary magazine, *Cobweb*. She is an editor and proofreader and writes occasional pieces for *The Irish Times*.

**Stephen Connolly** is from Belfast, where he is currently writing a Ph.D. in the Seamus Heaney Centre for Poetry. Some poems are forthcoming in *Poetry* (Chicago) and *The Irish Review*.

**David Cooke** won a Gregory Award in 1977. Widely published in the UK, Ireland and beyond, his most recent collection, *Work Horses*, was published in 2012 by Ward Wood Publishing. His next collection, *A Murmuration*, will be published by Two Rivers Press in 2015.

**Monica Corish**'s publication credits include *THE SHOp*, *Cyphers*, *The Stinging Fly* (including as Featured Poet, Spring 2009), *New Irish Writing*, *Southword*, *Orbis*, *The North*, *Causeway/Cabhsair* and *Artemis*. Her first collection, *Slow Mysteries*, was published by Doghouse Books (2012).

**Philip Cummins** is originally from Drumconrath, Co Meath. He is a graduate of Manchester Metropolitan University's MA in Creative Writing. Previously shortlisted for the Patrick Kavanagh Poetry Award, his poems have appeared in *Cyphers* and *The Burning Bush* 2. His arts criticism has appeared in *The Irish Post*, *NME* and online.

**Gerald Dawe** has published eight volumes of poetry with The Gallery Press, including *Selected Poems* (2012) and *Mickey Finn's Air* (2014). *The Stoic Man*, the final volume in his Lagan Press series of autobiographical and literary essays, is forthcoming, alongside a collection of *Early Poems*. He teaches at Trinity College, Dublin.

**Sien Deltour** attained her Masters in Literary Theory at the University of Leuven in 2013. Her main interest is contemporary Irish poetry, and she has done research on the work of Vona Groarke, Eiléan Ní Chuilleanáin and Sinéad Morrissey. She is currently working as coordinator for the European Federation of Associations and Centres of Irish Studies (EFACIS).

**Gearóid Denvir** was until recently Professor of Modern Irish at the National University of Ireland, Galway. He has published many books and articles in Irish, English and French on aspects of the Irish literary tradition, with a particular emphasis on modern literature. He has also published two volumes of poetry, *Iomramh Aigne* (1976) and *Trudaireacht* (1983).

**Edward Doegar**'s poems and reviews have appeared in various magazines including *Poetry Review*, *Poetry London*, *Ambit* and *Magma*. A selection of his work appears in the Bloodaxe anthology *Ten: The New Wave* (2014).

**Deirdre Doherty** is a Donegal-based poet. She has been published in *Crannóg*, *Neon Highway*, *The Stinging Fly*, *Black and Blue*, *The Moth* and *The Irish Independent*. In 2012 she was short-listed both for the Hennessy Poetry Prize (Emerging Poetry) and for the Bridport Prize.

**Susan Donnelly**'s latest collection is *Capture the Flag* (Iris Press, 2009). Her other books are *Eve Names the Animals*, *Transit*, and three chapbooks. She has published in *The New Yorker*, *Poetry*, and in many other journals, textbooks and anthologies. She lives, writes and teaches poetry in Arlington, Massachusetts, USA.

**Andrew Deloss Eaton,** born in California, now lives with his wife in Belfast. His poems and reviews appear in *Crab Orchard Review*, *Narrative*, *Magma* and *Pleiades*.

**Jonathan Ellis** teaches at Sheffield University. His most recent book is the edited collection, *Letter Writing Among Poets: From William Wordsworth to Elizabeth Bishop* (Edinburgh University Press, 2015).

**Andrew Fitzsimons** is the author of *The Sea of Disappointment: Thomas Kinsella's Pursuit of the Real* (UCD Press, 2008), and he edited *Thomas Kinsella: Prose Occasions* 1951-2001 (Carcanet, 2009). His latest poetry collection is *A Fire in the Head* (Isobar Press, 2014).

**Leontia Flynn**'s most recent collection is *Profit and Loss* (Cape Poetry, 2011). She won the AWB Vincent American Ireland Fund Literary Award in 2014.

**Miriam Gamble** is lecturer in Creative Writing at the University of Edinburgh. Her collections are *The Squirrels Are Dead* (2010) and *Pirate Music* (2014), both published by Bloodaxe Books.

**Lesley Harrison** lives and works on the North-East coast of Scotland. Her writing explores landscape and sense of place, through collaboration, myth, dialect and local history. Her most recent collection is *Beyond the Map* (Mariscat Press, 2012).

**Dermot Healy** (1947-2014) published novels, stories, a memoir and four collections of poetry. *The Travels of Sorrow* (The Gallery Press, 2015) gathers together his last poems.

**Lucy Ingrams** has poems published in various poetry magazines, both print and online. She has worked in gardens, schools, children's books publishing and a theatre company. Currently, she lives in Oxford, England.

**Hannah Jansen holds** a B.A. in English from the University of Vermont and an M.Phil. in creative writing from Trinity College, Dublin. Her writing has appeared in *Yew Journal, Naugatuck River Review* and *Albion Review*, among other outlets. A freelance editor, she is working on her first volume of poems.

**Biddy Jenkinson** is a poet, short story writer and dramatist. She is at present engaged in developing a bumblebee habitat in Wicklow. D'fhoilsigh Coiscéim *Táinrith*, 'cloch eile ar charn na Tána', i 2013.

**Maria Johnston** received her Doctorate in English Literature in 2007 and has since worked as a tutor and lecturer in Trinity College, Dublin, the Mater Dei Institute (DCU) and Oxford University. A well-known poetry critic, her reviews and essays have appeared in a range of publications including the *Guardian, Edinburgh Review, Poetry Review*, Tower Poetry's *Poetry Matters, The Oxford Handbook of Modern Irish Poetry* and *The Oxford Handbook of Contemporary British and Irish Poetry*.

**Richard Lambert** has had poems in the *Times Literary Supplement, The Spectator, Poetry Review, PN Review, The Rialto* and *THE SHOp*. A first collection, *Night Journey*, came out in 2012 (Eyewear Publishing).

**V P Loggins** is the author of *The Fourth Paradise* (Main Street Rag, 2010) and *Heaven Changes* (Pudding House Publications, 2007). He has also published one critical book on Shakespeare and is co-author of another. His poems and articles have appeared in *The Baltimore Review, Crannóg, The Dalhousie Review, The Healing Muse, Memoir, Poet Lore, The Southern Review* and *Third Wednesday*, among other journals.

**Catherine Phil MacCarthy**'s most recent collection, *The Invisible Threshold,* was published by Dedalus Press in 2012, and shortlisted for *The Irish Times* Poetry Now Award in 2013. She received the Fish International Poetry Prize in 2010, a residency at Centre Culturel Irlandais in Paris in 2013 and the O'Shaughnessy Award for Poetry in 2014. She is a former editor of *Poetry Ireland Review*.

**Thomas McCarthy** has published eight collections of poetry, including *The Sorrow Garden* (1981) and *The Last Geraldine Officer* (2009). A new collection, *Pandemonium*, is due from Anvil Press Poetry in late 2015. Winner of the Patrick Kavanagh and O'Shaughnessy Awards for poetry, as well as the Alice Hunt Bartlett Prize, he is a former editor of *Poetry Ireland Review* and a member of Aosdána.

**Jennifer A McGowan** obtained her Ph.D. from the University of Wales. Despite being certified as disabled at age 16, she has published poetry and prose in many magazines and anthologies on both sides of the Atlantic, including *The Rialto* and *The Connecticut Review.* Her chapbooks are available from Finishing Line Press; her first collection is forthcoming from Indigo Dreams.

**Patrick Maddock** is a former Hennessy Poetry Winner (2000) and he was shortlisted for the inaugural Gregory O'Donoghue International Poetry Competition. His work has appeared in various poetry magazines in Ireland and England.

**Jim Maguire** works as an adult education tutor in his native Wexford. A previous winner of the Strokestown International Poetry Prize, his first book of poems, *Music Field* (Poetry Salzburg, 2013), was shortlisted for the 2014 Shine/Strong Award.

**Geraldine Mitchell**'s second collection, *Of Birds and Bones*, was published by Arlen House in 2014. She won the Patrick Kavanagh Award in 2008. The poem published in this issue was placed third in the 2014 Strokestown International Poetry Competition.

Martin Monahan has recent work in *Ambit, Stand, The SHOp, The Rialto, PN Review, The Dublin Review, The White Review, The Threepenny Review, Poetry Magazine* and elsewhere. He is an Assistant Professor in Politics at the University of Nottingham.

Wendy Mooney lives in Dublin. She has previously had poems published in *Poetry Ireland Review, Crannóg, New Irish Writing, Authors and Artists* (Windows Publications), *10x3 plus, WOW! Magazine* and *College Green* (Trinity College, Dublin).

Tá seacht gcinn de chnuasaigh filíochta foilsithe ag **Dairena Ní Chinnéide**. Maireann sí i gCorca Dhuibhne lena mac Jeaic. She is currently working on her eighth collection, a bilingual publication with Dingle-based Ponc Press. A former broadcaster, television producer and interpreter, she has been concentrating on writing full-time for some years. Her most recent collection is *Cloithear: Aistear Anama* (Coiscéim, 2013).

Dan O'Brien, from New York, is a poet and playwright now living in Los Angeles. His *War Reporter* (CB Editions, 2013 / Hanging Loose Press, 2013) received the 2013 Fenton Aldeburgh First Collection Prize. *Scarsdale*, his second collection, was published by CB Editions in 2014 and will be published this year by Measure Press in the USA.

Hugh O'Donnell's latest collection is *No Place Like It* (Doghouse Books, 2010). A book of short reflections, *Songs for the Slow Lane*, is published by Columba Press (2015).

**Proinsias Ó Drisceoil** has written extensively on the literature and cultural history of Gaelic Ireland and Scotland. Publications include *Ar Scaradh Gabhail: An Fhéiniúlacht in Cín Lae Amhlaoibh Uí Shúilleabháin* (2000) and *Seán Ó Dálaigh: Éigse agus Iomarbhá* (2007). He was a contributor to the *New Oxford Dictionary of National Biography*, the *Encyclopedia of Ireland* and various other works of reference.

Oibríonn an Dr **Mícheál Ó hAodha** in Ollscoil Luimnigh. Mórán leabhar foilsithe aige as Gaeilge agus as Béarla, leabhair a scríobhadh faoi ainmneacha cleite san áireamh. Filíocht, gearrscéalta, iriseoireacht, leabhair taighde agus leabhair staire scríofa aige, go háirithe mar a bhaineann leis an Lucht Siúil, lucht oibre na hÉireann agus na Gaeil a thóg an bád bán orthu féin. Dhá bhailiúchán filíochta foilsithe aige: *Survivor/Dúchas Dóchasach* (2007) agus *Slán le hÉirinn* (2012).

**Liam Ó Muirthile** is a poet, novelist and dramatist. His most recent books are *An Fuíoll Feá: Rogha Dánta / Wood Cuttings: New and Selected Poems* (Cois Life, 2013) and the novel *An Colm Bán* (Cois Life, 2014).

Ciarán O'Rourke's poems have been featured in a number of publications, including *Crannóg*, *New Welsh Review*, *Poetry Review*, *The Irish Times*, *The Moth*, *The SHOp* and *The Spectator*. He was winner of the Lena Maguire/ Cúirt New Irish Writing Award in 2009, and his pamphlet *Some Poems* was issued as a *Moth Edition* in 2011.

Séamus Barra Ó Súilleabháin is a poet and spoken word artist from Listowel. He is currently working on a hip hop EP entitled *Craos*, as well as a collection of haiku. He was shortlisted for the 2015 People's Poetry Prize competition, and was the winner of the 2011 All Ireland Poetry Slam Competition.

Jocelyn Page is a poet from New England, currently living in South East London. Her pamphlet, *smithereens*, was published by the tall-lighthouse press in 2010. Her work has also appeared or is forthcoming in *Poetry Review*, *Poetry Salzburg*, *Smiths Knoll*, *The Rialto*, *Magma* and *The Moth*. Jocelyn is a final-year Ph.D. candidate at Goldsmiths College, London.

Ciarán Parkes lives in Galway. His poems have been published in *The Threepenny Review*, *The Rialto*, *The SHOp* and elsewhere.

Thomas Pirkle lives in Kinsale and has published poems in *Shenandoah*, *The Denver Quarterly* and other literary magazines.

Justin Quinn's book of poems *Early House* will be published this year by The Gallery Press. He works at the University of West Bohemia.

Billy Ramsell was awarded the Ireland Chair of Poetry Bursary in 2013. His most recent collection, *The Architect's Dream of Winter*, was short listed for *The Irish Times* Poetry Now Award.

Tadhg Russell lives in north Cork and has been writing poetry for the last number of years. His work has been published by *Southword*, *Cyphers*, *The Stony Thursday Book*, *New Irish Writing*, *West 47*, *The Stinging Fly*, *Atlanta Review* and *Solas Nua*. He made the shortlist for the Patrick Kavanagh Award in 2010.

Liam Ryan's debut collection *Touching Stones* was published by Doghouse Books in 2009. He was a prizewinner in the Strokestown International Poetry Competition in 2012, and is included in the Dublin Anthology *If Ever You Go* (Dedalus Press, 2014). A second collection is forthcoming.

John Sewell has published poems in various magazines and anthologies. His most recent collection is *Bursting The Clouds* (Cape Poetry). He lives in Bakewell, Derbyshire.

Gerard Smyth has published eight collections of poetry, including *A Song of Elsewhere* (Dedalus Press, 2015) and *The Fullness of Time: New and Selected Poems* (Dedalus Press, 2010). He is co-editor (with Pat Boran) of *If Ever You Go: A Map of Dublin in Poetry and Song* (Dedalus Press) which was Dublin's One City One Book in 2014. He is a member of Aosdána.

George Szirtes is a Hungarian-born British poet and translator. His most recent collection is *Bad Machine* (Bloodaxe Books, 2013).

Frances Corkey Thompson was born in Belfast and lives in Devon. Her work appears in many magazines and anthologies, including *Oxford Poets 2007* (Carcanet). Happenstance Press published her first chapbook, *The Long Acre*, in 2008, while this year Indigo Dreams will publish her first full collection, *Wild Gooseberries of Hailung*.

Jessica Traynor is a writer from Dublin. Her first collection, *Liffey Swim*, was published by Dedalus Press in 2014 and was shortlisted for the 2015 Strong/Shine Award.

Eoghan Walls lectures in Creative Writing at Lancaster University. He has received an Eric Gregory Award and an Irish Arts Council Bursary, and in 2012 his collection *The Salt Harvest* (Seren Books, 2011) was shortlisted for the Strong Award for Best First Collection. His next collection, *The Dance of Ararat*, is forthcoming.

Simon West is an Australian poet and Italianist. He is the author of two books of poetry, the most recent of which is *The Yellow Gum's Conversion* (Puncher and Wattmann, 2011), and an edition of the Italian poet Guido Cavalcanti.

David Wheatley lives in Aberdeenshire. His critical guide, *Contemporary British Poetry,* is published by Palgrave.

Anna Woodford's collection *Birdhouse* (Salt Publishing, 2010) won the Crashaw Prize and was a *Guardian* poetry book of the year. Her pamphlet *Party Piece* (Smith Doorstop, 2009) won the Poetry Business Competition and *Trailer* (Five Leaves, 2008) was a Poetry Book Society choice. She has a Ph.D. in the poetry of Sharon Olds.

Ocean Vuong's first full-length collection, *Night Sky With Exit Wounds*, will be published in 2016 by Copper Canyon Press. A 2014 Ruth Lilly fellow, he has received honours from Kundiman and Poets House, and is the recipient of a 2014 Pushcart Prize. His poems appear in *Poetry*, *The Nation* and *Boston Review*.